Secrets from Great Minds

John H. McMurphy, Ph.D.

Amaranth Publishing

Secrets from Great Minds

John H. McMurphy, Ph.D.

Published by:

Amaranth Publishing
P.O. Box 764167
Dallas, TX 75376

ISBN 0-9635487-9-4

Cover Art by Ryan Thrash Designs in Dallas

For information on John McMurphy's workshops, please call toll–free in the U.S. & Canada: (800) 321–2760

— DEDICATION —

To great minds from East and West...

I have devoted the past fifteen years to a search for "secrets from great minds," the universal wisdom from Eastern and Western cultures that assisted great minds in attaining their highest potential. This investigation led me through the journals, notebooks, autobiographies, and writings of many of the world's most creative artists, musicians, scientists, authors, philosophers, and spiritual leaders. I found that many great minds discovered specific techniques for unlocking their innate creativity, as well as profound ideas that inspired them to attain their full potential.

Because these great minds used universal wisdom to develop their own potential, I have been able to adapt their insights and techniques successfully to help a wide variety of contemporary audiences develop their creative potential, including:

- Southwestern Bell Telephone • Boston Society of Architects
- First Tennessee Bank System • The American Red Cross
- Office of the Mayor, City of Louisville, Kentucky
- Public and private schools in several states
- Adult learning centers across the country such as the Oasis Center in Chicago and Lily Dale in New York
- Adult education classes at Southern Methodist University, the University of Texas, the University of Louisville, Texas Christian University, and other educational institutions

Great minds discovered and used universal wisdom to unlock their full potential. They believed that we, too, can use this source to inspire our own journey towards self–realization. I dedicate this work to the profound example that great minds provided for us through their own journeys.

— John H. McMurphy, Ph.D.

– CONTENTS –

– contents continued –

– Preface –

OVERCOMING THE MOST COMMON RESISTANCES TO ENHANCING OUR HUMAN POTENTIAL

More than ten years experience teaching undergraduate and adult education classes as well as consulting with numerous individuals and business organizations has provided me with many insights into enhancing human potential and stimulating our innate creativity. One common assumption among the diverse people with whom I have worked is the perception that developing our innate human potential will be a monumental, if not altogether impossible, task. Some people even have offered reasons why they feel unable to develop their full potential. These perceptions, the most common of which are listed below, create formidable barriers to attaining our creative birthright. Yet, in spite of their initial resistance to developing their creative potential, most people with whom I have worked have learned a profound lesson: *The barrier lies within their resistance, not within their innate capabilities.*

Granted, our society may do little to encourage, and at times may discourage, developing our true creative potential; however, the great minds we will study in this book also faced personal and societal resistance to developing their creative potential. They learned to overcome whatever resistances they faced, and we can benefit from their experiences. The suggestions below, several of which have been adapted from the great minds themselves, have proven to be especially powerful tools for combatting any resistances to developing our creative potential. Before beginning the text, review these principles and techniques for removing any resistances you now may encounter. Refer to them again if you encounter resistance while discovering other secrets from great minds.

RESISTANCE # 1 "I'm just not very creative." – or – "I can't seem to realize my true potential."

1. The more you think or say this, the more it becomes your reality; it becomes a *self-fulfilling prophecy*. Learn to catch yourself thinking or saying this and immediately turn the thought around by thinking: "Until now, I just haven't fully activated my innate creative potential" - or - "I am developing my true human potential more each day" or similar affirmations that suggests awareness of your innate creative potential.

2. List your current activities that you consider to be creative or challenging, even if they may seem trivial or unimportant. Determine if any similarities exist between the activities you currently are performing and the activities performed by people you think are very creative or who have developed their potential to a high level. For example, you may be quite original in planning programs for your professional or civic association meetings. Compare this activity with how you think highly creative people approach their planning tasks. Look for similarities and acknowledge these as indications of your *present* creative ability. Then, in the future, affirm your present creative abilities whenever you feel the temptation to feel you are not creative.

RESISTANCE #2 "There's just not enough time to practice techniques to improve my creative potential."

1. Keep track of the time you spend practicing creative thinking and human development activities presented in this book for two weeks. Compare this time with the total time you spent in several other regular "spare-time" activities such as watching television, sports or recreational activities, exercise, reading, etc. What do

you notice? Is there any real reason to feel that you do not have enough time to develop your creative potential?

2. Research indicates, as do the journals of great minds, that as you practice the techniques and exercises to stimulate your innate creative potential, you will enhance your problem–solving abilities and increase your mental efficiency; therefore, consider the time you spend practicing creative thinking techniques to be an investment in yourself. A wise investment strategy is to tolerate small short–term sacrifices for substantial long–term gains. Your reward for devoting time now will be more NET available time in the future. Developing your creative potential pays large dividends, just as it has for the great minds.

RESISTANCE #3 "My job doesn't demand or allow for much creativity." – or – "My job doesn't present many opportunities to develop my full potential."

1. If this is your rationalization for not developing your creative potential, then you may have yielded to outdated assumptions about creativity in the business world. John Naisbitt and Patricia Aburdine in their book, *Re–inventing the Corporation*, present a future-oriented view of the business world's need for creative people. They maintain that in the coming global information age creative thinking skills will become a corporation's competitive edge in an increasingly competitive business environment. Already, more than half the Fortune 500 have implemented programs to develop employees' creative potential and to stimulate their problem–solving abilities. The evidence clearly indicates that creative thinking, rather than being limited to just a few occupations or segments of a business organization, will be an important survival skill for *all* businesses in the 21st century. The demand for creative thinkers will increase dramatically in the years ahead.

2. To feel that your present job does not demand much creativity also suggests that you may be overlooking opportunities to express yourself creatively. List the reasons you feel your job does not grant freedom for, or recognize the value of, creative thinking. As you use the secrets from great minds to stimulate and nurture your creative potential, these assumptions, most likely, will change. Practice the techniques to stimulate creative thinking for three weeks. Reevaluate the assumptions you previously listed. What do you notice? Keep track of your progress to provide feedback about your present opportunities to express your creative potential.

3. Transform your job so that it nurtures your true creative potential. My experience working with numerous individuals and business organizations has shown that one highly motivated person can stimulate significant transformation of his or her business organization. Use the insights gained from practicing the exercises and techniques in this book to lead you in this transformation. Be open to any possibilities! Great transformations often start with one inspired person who challenges society's assumptions (Newton, Edison, Galileo, Einstein, Picasso, Curie, da Vinci, *et al*). Also, you may find others in your organization awaiting someone to take the lead in transforming the organization.

4. Help your friends, family, and co–workers discover that activating our creative potential is no longer a luxury, but is a survival skill. Abraham Maslow, in his book *The Further Reaches of Human Nature*, observed that the future requires a "new human being," one who is fully creative. He believes that society must nurture such people if we are to survive the challenges that the future presents. Your lifestyle or job demands creativeness, even if you have not fully recognized its demands. All indications are that this demand will increase in the years ahead.

RESISTANCE # 4 "I'm just too logical and analytical to be more creative."

1. Again, this is a self-fulfilling prophecy. The more credence you grant it in your thoughts, the more it becomes your reality. Cease these thoughts immediately! Every time you catch yourself thinking this or similar thoughts, turn it around by saying: "Until now I've depended too much upon my analytical skills — but I don't have to do this anymore" -or- "My analytical skills serve some of my needs, while my more creative skills serve others."

2. Recognize that logical and rational thinking skills are NOT handicaps, but are valuable assets. List the ways you think highly creative and productive people would use these skills in both their creative and practical endeavors. Let this awareness temper your thoughts about your true creative potential.

3. Single out a trait or skill that you feel may limit your creativeness. For example, being too analytical and breaking problems down into minute parts may limit your potential. Pledge to forsake your chosen skill for a whole week. When you encounter a challenge or problem, do just the opposite of that trait. If you have forsaken breaking problems into small parts, then look for the "big picture." Notice how this changes your perspective about problems. Speculate whether this new approach to problem–solving could be useful in the future. If the problem remains unsolved after using your new trait, explore the reasons why. Do you simply require more practice with this newly acquired asset or do you need to return to your previously mastered skill? Remember to give yourself adequate time and practice when learning to use new skills.

→ *Consider this time and effort to be an investment in your future.*

RESISTANCE #5 "I'm afraid to develop my creativity because my life might change."

1. Discover the value of change in our lives. Henri Bergson, in his Nobel Prize acceptance speech observed that: "For a conscious being, to exist is to change, to change is to mature, to mature is to go on creating oneself endlessly." Change, rather than being a destructive force, is a creative and life–enriching force; it stimulates us to reach our highest potential. We really should fear that our lives *do not* change.

2. Determine if your resistance to change is a fear of improving your potential or simply a fear of unknowns? List all the things that would be, or you feel might be, different about your life if you suddenly became more creative and productive than you are now. Explore each of these potential differences. Is it really something to fear? How could this change be useful and rewarding to you? To others? What does this tell you?

3. Explore the creativity of prominent civic and business leaders you know either personally or through other means. List the characteristics and attributes you feel are responsible for their creativeness. Are these traits something to fear? How has possessing these traits affected these civic and business leaders? Would you benefit by possessing these attributes? How?

> **Remember this premise as you probe the secrets from great minds:** *Great minds are "great" largely because they overcame the major resistances to improving their innate human potential.*

Fortunately, they have provided us with many techniques and insights that will assist in our own self–realization efforts. This book presents several of the most powerful techniques great minds such as da Vinci, Edison,

Emerson, Tennyson, Jung, Thoreau, and Socrates used to overcome resistances to developing their full human potential. If you now experience any resistance to developing your human potential to higher levels, or if as you read this book you encounter such barriers, use the *Secrets from Great Minds* as your guide.

Great Minds	Techniques Presented
Leonardo da Vinci	The Renaissance Rorschach
Jean Dubuffet	A Child's Eye–View
Marcel Duchamp	The Questioning Techniques
Thomas Edison	Idea Files
Ralph Waldo Emerson	Make Your Own Bible
Max Ernst	Collage Creation
Johann Wolfgang von Goethe	Describe Out Loud
Carl Jung	Inner Guide Visualization
Paul Klee	Kleevision
Joan Miró	Collage Creation
Claes Oldenberg	A Child's Eye–View
Robert Rauschenberg	Collage Creation
Percy Bysshe Shelley	Camera Obscura Visualization
Socrates	The Questioning Techniques
Alfred, Lord Tennyson	Nuclear Shorthand
Henry Thoreau	Keeping a Journal
Jean Tingueley	Collage Creation
J. M. W. Turner	A Child's Eye–View
James Whistler	Describe Out Loud
Walt Whitman	Idea Files

Additional inspiration for the techniques comes from: Mozart, van Gogh, Beethoven, Wagner, Fuller, Einstein, Maslow, Blake, Buddha, Newton, Hardy, Twain, St. Teresa of Avila, Cézanne, and James.

HOW TO DERIVE THE MOST BENEFIT FROM THIS BOOK

Secrets from Great Minds has several goals that affect its organization and content. Please bear these goals in mind as you read the text.

• **You are part of the process** — This book contains two levels of "secrets" from great minds. First, there are many techniques the great minds actually used to stimulate their own creative potential. You may derive similar benefits as you incorporate their techniques into your own self–realization activities. Second, there are twenty-one chapters in Part Two presenting inspirational wisdom generated by great minds. These secrets can help us understand our world and our relationship with it.

Rather than spelling out in detail the potential meaning of these twenty–one secrets, I have prepared only a small opening commentary. This gives you the freedom to construct the secret's full meaning through reading, contemplation, and exploration. It also places much of the responsibility for learning upon you. The more actively you engage yourself in the learning process, the greater will be your potential benefit from this book. If you enhance the ability to probe classical wisdom through this process, then you can study other texts to glean their secrets as well. As Carl Rogers maintains, only those who have *learned how to learn* are prepared for the future.

• **The great mind's techniques and exercises will help reveal the secrets** — Many techniques and exercises actually used by the great minds are included in the text. Practicing these activities will help integrate the secrets into your daily needs, just as it did for the great minds originally responsible for the activities.

• Proceeding slowly enhances your experience — There is no need to rush through this text. Moving slowly through each technique or secret and allowing it to blossom in your mind is more beneficial than completing it quickly. Spending a day exploring each technique or quotation could be an appropriate way to progress through the secrets. Let your intuitive wisdom guide your progress. *Whenever* you feel that you have discovered either a technique's or an entire secret's essential meaning, then proceed forward.

• The secrets have been placed in an order to promote understanding — You are certainly free to explore the secrets in any fashion your intuitive wisdom suggests; however, if you do not feel "led" by your intuition to depart from the order in which they are presented, then follow the order given in the text.

• Record your thoughts in a journal to promote understanding — Great minds kept journals, and so must we. The journal will be your greatest ally as you explore the secrets. If you need assistance with keeping a journal, refer to the Activator technique on page 22 in the *Introduction*.

• Finally, remember this advice as you study the *Secrets from Great Minds*:

"Ultimate truth, if there be any such thing, requires the concert of many voices."

Carl Jung, *Collected Works, Volume 18*

WHAT IS A "GREAT MIND?"

There are always in the world a few inspired people who spring up.

Plato, *Laws*

Through the ages, many great minds have surfaced on this planet in various time periods and geographic locations. These people have uncovered fundamental secrets about the human condition and the universe itself, and they have recorded their discoveries for the benefit of future generations. Their discoveries bear many striking similarities to each other despite enormous differences among the great minds in time, space, lifestyle, and means of expression. Some came from Eastern cultures while others came from the West. Some great minds, such as Marcus Aurelius, Tennyson, Tolstoy, and Mencius, lived rather affluently at times, while others, such as Schweitzer, Gandhi, Socrates, and Buddha disavowed an affluent lifestyle. Whereas some spoke openly of the universal source from which they drew their inspiration, others merely alluded to that source. The means they chose to express their discoveries are as diverse as the great minds themselves: philosophy, art, spirituality, music, medicine, writing, and science. These great minds, simply because they developed their mental and spiritual capabilities far beyond that of others around them, seemed to have been extraordinarily exceptional human beings.

Were these great minds aberrations in the human population? Were they endowed with special abilities and genius denied to the vast human multitude? Did these great minds enter realms of awareness that most people only dream about or long to experience themselves? Can the average person access, understand, and utilize these secrets to develop his or her highest mental and spiritual potential as the great minds have done? This book addresses these and other questions about what constitutes a "great mind" and how each of us may learn from their experiences. Our journey begins with recent discoveries about humanity's true creative potential.

UNIVERSAL HUMAN POTENTIAL

Scientists have shown that it is possible for almost anyone to experience creative breakthroughs.

Willis Harman, *Higher Creativity*

Numerous scientific and psychological breakthroughs during recent decades have shattered the notion of "genius" as being a rare, infrequent occurrence among human beings. Among the first tremors that rocked the genius concept was Dr. Charles Hulbreck's 1943 address before the New York Academy of Medicine in which he encouraged his colleagues to accept "the decline of the genius concept and the replacement of talent and gift with the term creativeness." Dr. Hulbreck spoke for many others who were beginning to realize that creative inspiration was not "a gift from the gods" as it was thought to be in ancient Greece. Nor was it as a "gift of birth" that was reserved for a few very fortunate individuals as it came to be known during the Renaissance. Instead, the modern perspective hailed creative inspiration as a universal human birthright, an innate characteristic. This means that we, like the great minds, share this potential.

Sigmund Freud's work at the turn of the century provided the impetus for the movement away from the "genius" explanation and towards the understanding that tremendous untapped potential is universal among human beings. His exploration of the human mind revealed numerous mental activities that appeared to be available for purposes other than our ordinary daily activities. William James took Freud's lead and found mental activities constantly occurring outside what he called our "normal waking consciousness." Soon science developed the technological means to map and chart these previously unexplored mental realms. The result has confirmed the view that creative potential is not limited to a few chosen people like the great minds; rather, it is a universal human experience. In other words, each of us has the potential to become a "great mind."

Me, A Great Mind?

Dr. Susan Fisher's research at the University of Chicago indicates that we now must look beyond terms such as "talent" or "genius" and see that all humanity has an unlimited capacity for creative growth. Psychologist Abraham Maslow's extensive study of creative, self-actualizing people led him to the same conclusion. He even describes creative potential as a "fundamental characteristic inherent in human nature." You may be wondering whether you will need a certain "intelligence level" to claim your potential. The answer is a resounding "NO!" David Perkins' research at Harvard demonstrates that numerous people possessing fairly average intelligence, and even many with less than average intelligence, have enhanced their creative potential significantly.

For all practical purposes, virtually everyone has the potential for tapping his or her innate creative resources and accessing the same secrets as did the great minds. Then, once we have accessed these secrets, we can apply this wisdom to developing our mental and spiritual potential to the highest levels. No longer should we feel that we lack the talent or mental ability to lead creative, spiritually fulfilling lives. Remember:

Reaching our full potential depends far more upon applying ourselves to the process than upon talent or intellectual endowment.

HOW GREAT MINDS DEVELOPED

- • **Broad Knowledge**
- • **Synthesis of Knowledge**
- • **Awareness of the Present Moment**
- • **Universal Sources of Knowledge**
- • **Great Minds had Techniques**

Broad Knowledge

Probe the universe in a myriad points...He is a wise man who has taken many views.

Henry David Thoreau, *Journals*

Great minds avidly explored the human knowledge base and drew inspiration from each other. Many great minds, especially in the West, received a "classical education" that emphasized certain luminary texts (*The Homeric Hymns*, Aeschylus' *Agamemnon*, Plato's *Republic*, Aristotle's *Rhetoric*, Seneca's *Epistles*, and St. Thomas' *Summa Theologica* being but a few examples) as being the foundation of human wisdom. These venerable works contained many of the "secrets" discovered during ancient explorations, and people who studied these classical texts, therefore, had access to these timeless ideas. Unfortunately, our modern educational system often dismisses or barely touches upon the ancient wisdom available to us. Today, if we desire to understand and utilize the secrets generated by great minds, then many of us will need to broaden our classical knowledge base and expose ourselves to these universal ideas. This book presents a starting point for this objective; however, broad–based knowledge alone will not suffice, for as the great minds realized, knowledge exists as a synthesis of great ideas.

Synthesis of Knowledge

Making variations on a theme is really the crux of creativity.

Douglas Hofstadter, *Metamagical Themas*

Throughout history, great minds have demonstrated the ability to synthesize and transform the knowledge they discovered into new creations for others to share. Great ideas at any point in time will exist in a dynamic interrelationship with other ideas — both classical and contemporary. For example, Francis Bacon transformed Aristotle's inductive thinking method into a new framework important in modern scientific analysis, and Thoreau and Emerson incorporated ancient Hindu and Buddhist ideas into their Transcendental Ideal. Frank Lloyd Wright united Japanese Temple design principles with his own ideas to create his spacious, airy *Prairie Home*, and the divergent ideas of Charles Darwin and Goethe affected Sigmund Freud early in his life. Profound knowledge does not exist as isolated fragments of a larger whole; rather, *it is the whole*. Great minds have discovered how to interrelate and synthesize the fragments of knowledge they encounter into the whole known as universal wisdom.

An Encounter with the Present Moment

The surest way to create something is losing oneself in the present, being inspired by the surroundings, yielding to what is directly before oneself.

Vincent van Gogh, *Letters*

Rollo May's book, *The Courage to Create*, describes the capacity to become fully absorbed in our present life experiences as having an "encounter" with reality, a factor crucial to creative endeavors as van Gogh indicates. An encounter occurs when we focus our awareness upon some object or experience to such an extent that we seem to become "one" with the object; anything other than what lies before us consequently fades from our awareness. Because we mentally unite with the object or experience during an encounter, we produce numerous insights that a less–focused glance may have overlooked. An encounter, according to Martin Buber, also helps us transform an object before us from simply being an "it" into being a "Thou." In other words, an encounter nurtures reverence for whatever objects or experiences cross our path. This not only enriches appreciation for our seemingly mundane experiences, but it also furnishes us with insights useful in our creative and self–realization activities.

Abraham Maslow maintains that having encounters with life experiences is a common characteristic of great minds. His study of creative, self–actualizing people led him to this conclusion:

> The creative person, in the inspirational phase of the creative furor, loses his past and future and lives only in the moment. He is all there, totally immersed, fascinated, and absorbed in the present, in the current situation, in the here and now, with the matter at hand.

Any distraction such as focusing upon our past or future activities, idle daydreaming, paying attention to physiological stirrings (hunger, tiredness, sleepiness, physical discomfort, etc.), or even environmental factors such as noise or excitement may prevent an encounter. As children, however, our encounters with objects and life experiences could so thoroughly engage our attention that, for the moment, they were our total reality. Distractions such as parents calling our name, nightfall's arrival, the school bell ringing, our stomach growling, etc. often did not interrupt our fascination with whatever had captured our attention. We, as children, were having encounters similar to the ones that great minds have experienced.

Somehow, as adults, distractions that we overlooked as children creep into our mind with greater ease, thereby thwarting potentially meaningful encounters with our life experiences. Perhaps, because we feel that we have already "learned" all that we need to "know" about the world, we perceive little need to have new encounters. Or, maybe as adults, we believe that our primary objective is to cope with reality and that potential encounters such as stopping to smell the heliotropes, gazing at the sun's prismatic reflection in a puddle of water, or listening to a Spring rainfall are experiences more suitable for poets and artists. We must recognize that having genuine encounters with our immediate life experiences, rather than being a waste of time or sheer folly, is the foundation for developing our full human potential. Great minds consistently demonstrate this awareness.

Universal Sources of Knowledge and Inspiration

One after another the greatest writers, poets, and artists confirm the fact that their work comes to them from beyond the threshold of consciousness.

Percy Bysshe Shelley, *A Defence of Poetry*

One prevalent theme among Eastern thinkers concerns the *local* and *universal* aspects of the human mind. The local, or small, mind (what we in the West understand best as the logical–rational conscious mind) is indigenous to the person; it is his or her unique creation. The local mind is blank at birth which means that we must construct its contents from our experiences and our reactions to them as we mature. Abraham Maslow calls the logical and rational processes the local mind uses to construct its contents "secondary processes," because they are not present at birth but are learned from those around us already using these processes. Since we use logical, rational processes to construct the local mind's contents and perform its basic operations, its understanding is limited to those ideas or things it perceives to be logical or rational. The local mind often rejects or dismisses any seemingly illogical or irrational ideas (intuitive insights, for example) it encounters, thereby causing us to lose potentially valuable resources for self–improvement.

The local mind, by limiting us to those ideas or experiences its secondary processes can understand, is simply too prosaic to provide us with the inspiration necessary to develop our full human potential. It is similar to what William James referred to as the "ordinary waking consciousness," because it directs and controls our routine daily activities. Thoughts such as: "I need to go to the grocery store," "The company has a cash flow problem," and "Tonight's sunset was lovely" typify the local mind's agenda. The local mind copes with ordinary, everyday reality which renders it an inadequate source for developing either creative inspiration or profound knowledge.

The local mind presents another limitation to developing our full potential. While each of our local minds possesses some similarity in content and operation, each one, since we created it ourselves, is entirely unique. Anytime we communicate (either by written, oral, or artistic means) with each other using only the local mind's perspective and capabilities, the sender and receiver experience similar, yet never precisely the same, meaning. What one person understands to be "honor," "truth," or "beauty" may be very close to, but not the same as, what another person may understand those terms to mean. For example, Plato's reference to "justice" in his *Republic* connotes a substantially different understanding from Thomas Hobbes' use of the term in *Leviathan*. Likewise, what one person understands either the color "red" or "bold vertical lines" to mean in art may not be another person's understanding. The local mind truly understands only itself, and this is a potentially serious barrier to gleaning wisdom from the great minds' ideas. We must dedicate ourselves to removing this potential barrier, if we are to enhance our innate creativity.

Leaving the Local Mind

To communicate ideas and insights effectively, either between each other or between the great minds and ourselves, we occasionally must bypass the local mind's limitations discussed above and develop modes of awareness more appropriate for the task. Fortunately, we can transcend the local mind's limitations and experience enhanced awareness as C.M. Cade indicates in his book, *The Awakened Mind:*

> It is very difficult to grasp the concept that our so-called normal waking state is neither the highest nor the most efficient state of which we are capable. There are other states of mind of vastly greater awareness which we can enter and then return to normal living enriched, enlivened and enhanced.

"What are these states?" and "How can I find universal wisdom?" may be among the questions running through your mind right now. Twenty–five hundred years ago, similar questions may have led Greek philosopher Heraclitus to his conclusion that universal wisdom *necessarily* must come from the universal element present in us all, not from our local or individual faculties. Through the centuries, as Shelley indicates, many other great minds understood the need to transcend the local mind and venture to the realms "beyond the threshold of consciousness" to obtain their creative inspiration. One of the secrets from great minds elaborates on Shelley's statement.

Discover the Universal Mind

The universal mind is what many Westerners have called the intuitive or transcendent mind, and it bears resemblance to the collective unconscious described by Carl Jung. The universal mind's contents, unlike that of the local mind, is not our own creation. It is omniscient and transcends all matter, time, and space. The universal mind remains outside the local mind's awareness for the most part; however, it can reveal the universe's secrets to the local mind by direct apprehension of universal truths. If we tap the universal mind, we can harvest universal, transcendental wisdom. (Refer to Aristotle's ideas that follow). Once we have access to this wisdom, we can use it for creative inspiration or for our self–development. As you will discover when reading the chapters that follow, great minds consistently accessed the universal mind, even if they did not always directly attribute their inspiration to this source. Just as the great minds drew inspiration from universal sources, so can we.

ARISTOTLE ON DISCOVERING UNIVERSAL TRUTH

There are four ways we discover truth

1) Scientific reasoning — using experimentation to create and test hypotheses

2) Practical reasoning — using practical reasoning and common sense

3) Philosophical reasoning — using logical argumentation and reasoning

4) Intuitive Reasoning — direct, intuitive apprehension of truth

Aristotle maintains that while any of the first three can lead us to truth, intuitive reason, because it is direct apprehension of truth and not subject to potentially faulty logic or reasoning, is the only means to reach UNIVERSAL TRUTHS (truths that exist outside human logic and reasoning, truths sought by the great minds).

Aristotle, *Nicomachean Ethics*

To receive inspiration from a universal source requires that we actively cultivate the universal mind and become comfortable with its nature. Unfortunately, the local mind, since it directs and controls virtually every waking minute, does not relish the idea of relinquishing its control to an unknown or unfamiliar source such as the universal mind. It will take concerted effort and much patience to cultivate the universal mind and to help the local mind feel less threatened by what it perceives to be a competing entity. To overcome this obstacle, great minds have used various forms of contemplative meditation.

Contemplative meditation is the key. It allows us to transfer awareness from the local mind to the universal mind in small steps so we diminish the local mind's anxiety. Once we gradually have calmed the local mind's uncertainty about relinquishing control and have transferred awareness to the universal mind, we can begin to receive wisdom from the universal source. Although this may sound alien to many of us, these processes have helped produce much of the world's greatest art, music, poetry, writing, and even scientific achievements. Great minds are "great" largely because their minds are universal minds, minds open to the universal truths to which Aristotle refers. The following section describes their methods for developing openness to universal inspiration.

Great Minds Had Techniques

Creatively productive people do, in every case, develop and use personal creative thinking techniques.

Gary Davis

Creativity researcher Gary Davis reveals an astonishing insight about creative people — *they consistently develop and use techniques to spur creative thinking.* Why would creative people have to devise techniques to provide inspiration for their works? It is simply because our ordinary mental activities are not suited for generating creative or universally relevant ideas. The local or conscious mind, since it is entirely our own creation, is best suited to "manage" our lives, not seek inspirational ideas or universal wisdom. Ordinary waking consciousness is, as the name implies, *ordinary*. To develop their highest mental and spiritual potential, great minds occasionally had to lead themselves out of their local mind in order to receive input from the universal mind. For this purpose, they developed and used specific techniques.

The techniques great minds used are not basic skills such as techniques for holding the brush or techniques to produce interesting plot combinations. Almost without exception, they developed techniques to alter their awareness so they could be more open to universal creative inspiration. Examples of these consciousness-shifting techniques include:

•Sir Isaac Newton gazed at the stars for hours on end and found himself able to enter a dreamlike, yet comprehensible mental state where many of his best ideas took shape.

•Beethoven, Emerson, and Wagner took long walks through the woods with no other purpose than to leave ordinary awareness behind and experience universal awareness.

•Alfred, Lord Tennyson repeated his own name to himself until he entered a trancelike state where he found many creative ideas for his poetry. (Today we would say that Tennyson used his name as a *mantra*).

•Shelley sat by lakes and allowed the water's scintillation to induce a dreamy state of awareness in which his poetic ideas took shape.

•Leonardo da Vinci often looked at cracked floors, paint-spattered walls, or dried clay to stimulate his imagination to "see" various items among these rather ordinary subjects.

•Artist Paul Klee altered his ordinary vision by placing binoculars, antique glass, or similar items between himself and his subject, so the distorted images he saw could liberate his perception and stimulate new ideas about the subject.

•William Wordsworth would sit by the fireside and gaze at the burning logs until they mesmerized him into a state of lucid imagination which produced insights for his writing.

These are but a few of the techniques great minds actually used to liberate themselves from the handicap of ordinary, local consciousness. They did not have the scientific knowledge generated by modern sophisticated electronic mind–scanning technologies (PET or CAT scanners) or the psychological understanding gained by Carl Jung, Abraham Maslow, Carl Rogers, and other pioneers of the human psyche. Long before anyone really understood creativity's biological and psychological elements, these great minds *intuitively knew* how to stimulate their minds. Remarkably, these earlier, intuitively developed techniques contain the basic principles that we now know can help liberate our innate human potential. Several techniques great minds used will follow in the next section. Other of their techniques can be found in Part Three.

HOW TO USE THIS BOOK

1. Invest in Yourself

2. Become Part of the Process

3. Use the ACTIVATORS
   ◊ **Make Your Own Bible—Ralph Waldo Emerson**
   ◊ **Keep a Journal — Henry David Thoreau**
   ◊ **Idea Files — Thomas Edison and Walt Whitman**
   ◊ **Nuclear Shorthand — Alfred, Lord Tennyson**
   ◊ **The Questioning Techniques — Marcel Duchamp & Socrates**

4. Practice the Techniques and Exercises

5. Share — Network — Utilize the Secrets

6. Develop Meditate Awareness

There are several ways you may use this book to probe the secrets from great minds. *How* you approach the task will determine, to a substantial degree, what you will discover. If your goal is to develop an acquaintance with great minds from Eastern and Western civilizations, then a casual reading of the texts will suffice. If, on the other hand, you wish to penetrate to the essence of these secrets and incorporate their wisdom into your life, then you will need a more substantive and comprehensive study. The following are suggestions to help you probe these secrets and integrate the wisdom contained within them into your life.

1. Invest in Yourself

Genius is not a function of genes or hormonal influences. *Genius is process.* It is correlated to the individual's life cycle. Genius is dependent upon what the individual is doing or is determined to do with his or her native endowment.

Jan Ehrenwald, *Anatomy of Genius*

If Ehrenwald is correct, and much research confirms his point, then what we do, *or what we do not do*, with our native endowment will determine how far we progress towards realizing our true human potential. If reaching your full human potential is as important to you as it was to the great minds, then you must actively pursue this goal and dedicate sufficient resources to its attainment. This will require time and effort on your part, but what could possibly be a more appropriate use of your time than to progress towards your true potential?

"How much time?" or "How can I afford the time with my busy schedule?" are questions you may be asking yourself right now. Naturally, the answer depends upon your motivation, your willingness to pursue new paths, and how relevant you perceive the secrets from great minds to be in your daily activities. Consider the time and effort you spend as an investment in yourself. As with any investment, the net yield reflects the performance of the chosen investment activities. Strong performances produce high net yields; therefore, your dedication to the process determines your rewards. Potential rewards include: improved thinking skills, greater mental flexibility, enhanced spirituality, fewer distractions caused by fears or anxieties, improved communication abilities, and a deeper sense of purpose in life. Thus, attaining your true potential may actually generate a *net increase* in time available for this process and for your other daily activities.

Overcoming the "mental inertia" to start this process will, most likely, be your greatest task; however, once you begin, the momentum you generate through your discoveries should be sufficient to sustain your progress. Initially commit one hour a day to the development of your full human abilities. You may spend this hour among different self–improvement activities: reading the great minds' ideas, keeping a journal, meditating, sharing the insights you have discovered with others, or performing the exercises and activities that follow. Remember, the hardest part is to get moving, so make the commitment to invest in yourself.

2. Become part of the process

Eastern masters tell anyone seeking wisdom or enlightenment that "the journey is the goal." In other words, the *process* of seeking wisdom is as valuable as any wisdom that we can obtain through our search. If you desire to understand wisdom from great minds, realize that the actual process you use to discover their ideas, *your personal journey*, will be as important as any wisdom you encounter. For this reason, rather than spelling out in detail the potential meaning of each secret, this book presents only a small opening remark before each secret. This gives you the freedom to construct each secret's meaning in personal terms through reading, contemplation, and exploration. This, by the way, was the method great minds used in their journey.

Obtaining insight acquired through one's personal efforts requires that you become an active participant in the learning process. The more actively you engage yourself in the learning process, the greater will be your potential benefit. If you experience difficulty, rely upon the ACTIVATORS for assistance. They will strengthen your ability to glean insights from the great minds' thoughts, ideas, and techniques. If you strengthen your ability to probe classical wisdom through this process, then you will have taught yourself "how to learn." As Carl Rogers maintains, only those who have *learned how to learn* are prepared adequately for the future. Enjoy the journey!

3. Use The ACTIVATORS

The ACTIVATORS will become a trusted ally as you strive to develop your mental and spiritual potential. They are powerful techniques actually created by great minds to discover interrelationships among ideas, to probe themselves for new ideas, and to synthesize their discoveries into new insights for themselves and others.

The ACTIVATORS also incorporate a basic principle from Carl Jung's methods to help his clients realize their full human potential. Jung found that anytime he could get his clients to utilize insights gleaned from their inner world in their daily lives, they would derive significantly greater benefit than if they had simply become aware of the insight. He deduced that taking action upon the insight not only reinforced their ability to integrate these insights into their lives, but it also gave clients more access to their inner world. If we, too, can integrate new insights into our lives and provide greater access to our inner world, then we will improve our self–realization efforts substantially.

The four techniques which follow incorporate the activation principle. They encourage us to explore and activate on the conscious level the insights and ideas that our study and readings will provide us. As you explore the ideas presented by the great minds in this book, use the ACTIVATORS to obtain greater perspective upon their ideas and also to integrate these new perspectives into your future studies and life activities. The ACTIVATORS also can provide valuable assistance if you experience difficulty with any particular idea. Practice each one until you feel comfortable with it and try using them in combination with each other as you encounter new ideas.

ACTIVATOR: Make Your Own Bible — Ralph Waldo Emerson

GOAL: To use thoughts and ideas from great minds as a means of personal inspiration. To create a reference tool for use in studying classical wisdom.

Ralph Waldo Emerson recorded a helpful piece of advice for us in his journals. He recommends that we create our own "Bible" which will become a source of personal inspiration for us and will help us gain better perspective upon the ideas others have produced. He writes: "Make your own Bible. Select and collect all the words and sentences that come to you like the blast of the trumpet." Emerson understands that insightful words or ideas from others can inspire our own minds to greater things. He faithfully read his Personal Bible to expand his understanding and provide ideas for his writing.

Thomas Hardy, another prominent American writer, likewise found that collecting interesting ideas enhanced his thinking. Hardy kept numerous notebooks containing fragments of thought, highlights from conversations, interesting metaphors, tidbits from scientific journals, and other items he called, "trifles of knowledge," which were sources of inspiration for him. In fact, there are more than twenty specific uses of these ideas from his notebooks in *The Return of the Native*. These "trifles of knowledge" also found their way into many other of Hardy's works.

Often, in our reading or conversation, we encounter an idea which triggers something deep inside us to recognize the idea as having profound importance. If we consider the idea briefly and then proceed onward with our other activities, then we may miss a golden opportunity to incorporate that wisdom into our lives. Great minds cannot communicate their wisdom to us if we fail to explore their ideas adequately. We must let their wisdom synthesize with other ideas we have encountered to increase our understanding.

One way to explore great ideas is to record and investigate, as did Emerson, Hardy, and many others, those ideas that hit you like the blast of a trumpet. The Personal Bible is the perfect device for exploring any thoughts or ideas that you find important. Recording and investigating ideas will require some effort on your part; however, the effort will be repaid immeasurably. As you read the selections from great minds in this book or from other sources, enter the ones that grab your attention in your Personal Bible. Your efforts not only will help activate the ideas, but will also produce a valuable reference tool for future studies. Steps for creating your Personal Bible are:

1. Find a bound blank book. Artist supply stores usually are a good source. You may decorate or personalize it.

2. Determine how you want to record and access your "found" ideas. Suggestions include:

Subject Indexing — Determine in advance the subjects you might wish to include in your bible. Devote what you feel to be an appropriate number of pages for each subject area. Mark your pages and record your ideas accordingly. To include ideas not in your original subject determination, have a miscellaneous section. This book, in fact, grew from my Personal Bible that is indexed by subject matter.

Author Indexing — Perhaps there are a few great minds on whom you want to focus your Personal Bible. Devote an appropriate number of pages to those authors and record their ideas accordingly.

Chronological Indexing — This method focuses upon studying ideas from particular time periods (e.g., American Transcendentalism, the Golden Age of Athens, Romanticism). Determine your interests and devote sufficient pages for each era.

3. Explore ideas as you record them. You may need to investigate other books and materials to grasp the essence of the newly found idea. Try using questions such as the following to facilitate your understanding.

•Why did the person come to this conclusion? Is it consistent with thoughts from other great minds? Why or why not?

•Are there other ideas that are prerequisites for understanding this idea? What are they, and where can I find them?

•What were the circumstances that prompted the person to express this idea?

•Does this idea address more than the author's own generation? Does it still apply to human needs? If so, how?

•How can this idea be combined with other ideas to offer even more insight?

•How can I apply this idea to my present needs?

4. After investigating the idea, record any new thoughts or perspectives that are triggered by your exploration of great ideas in your journal. These new perspectives may

contain elements of your own intuitive wisdom and should be recorded for later use or exploration.

5. **Read your Bible.** Refer to it often to see if previously explored ideas generate new perspectives as you review your Bible.

ACTIVATOR: Keep a Journal — Henry David Thoreau

Consider Thoreau's thoughts on keeping a journal:

We should not endeavor cooly to analyze our thoughts, but, keeping the pen even and parallel with the current, make an accurate transcript of them. Impulse is, after all, the best linguist.

Journal, 1838

My journal is a record of the mellow and ripe moments that I would keep. I do not preserve the husk of life, but the kernel.

Journal, 1851

I keep a journal which should contain those thoughts and impressions which I am most liable to forget that I had.

Journal, 1851

I can hardly believe that there is so great a difference between one year and another as my journal shows.

Journal, 1851

Time never passes so rapidly as when I am engaged in recording my thoughts.

Journal, 1852

Virtually any great mind could present the merits of keeping a journal, because virtually all great minds have kept a journal or record of their thoughts and ideas. Henry David Thoreau, however, not only *kept* a journal, he did it with an almost unparalleled passion and zeal. Thoreau's *Journals*, an extraordinary collection containing more than two million words, are America's most extensive record of one person's life experiences. Quantity was not his only strength, as Martin Buber indicates: "By speaking as concretely as he does about his own historical situation, Thoreau expresses exactly that which is valid for all human history." Thoreau, perhaps the exemplary journal–keeper, will be our guide for keeping a journal.

Thoreau's own ideas on keeping a journal, a few of which are given above, indicate to us several incentives for keeping our own journal:

- To stimulate more thought by writing down our ideas
- To stimulate immediate "intuitive" impressions
- To encourage self-knowledge
- To avoid judgment of our thoughts before we have had time to express them fully
- To harvest the choice ideas (the "kernels") from our many life experiences
- To provide a permanent record of our thoughts, so we do not lose them through time
- To provide perspective on our thoughts and lives as we review prior journal entries
- To promote awareness of the present moment
- To engage ourselves in an engrossing, rewarding activity

Researchers have found that keeping a journal actually stimulates and nurtures the processes listed above, largely because journal keeping promotes self–awareness and a broader perspective on our lives. Keeping a journal also will give us greater access to the secrets that great minds offer. Emerson's technique, **Make Your Own Bible**, will provide you with a collection of quotations, thoughts, and ideas that various great minds through the ages have produced. Your journal, however, will be a collection of *your own* thoughts, ideas, and impressions. As discussed below, your journal also will be an excellent location to record your thoughts about and reactions to the exercises in this book. For these reasons, keeping a journal contributes substantially to our making progress in life's journey.

Suggestions for Keeping a Journal

Use the following suggestions if you have little experience in keeping a journal or if you desire to expand your present journal–keeping to include studying the wisdom great minds have provided us. Initially, until journal–keeping becomes a familiar and comfortable experience, commit yourself to making daily journal entries, no matter how small or trivial they seem. Remember, your journal is a spontaneous reflection upon your own life experiences; therefore, it is important to maintain an open mind and avoid judgment and criticism of your entries. Through time, you most likely will find that a commitment is no longer needed, because keeping a journal will have become a stimulating and rewarding activity. Use your imagination and trust your hunches as you try the suggestions listed below.

Journal Suggestions for Bringing the Great Minds into Your Life

1. Write letters to one or more great minds that:

- will ask questions and seek advice
- will offer your comments, suggestions, and feedback to the great mind
- will tell the person how an idea he or she produced has affected you

- will ask how a great mind's most important obser-vations developed
- will show how you have related one of the great mind's ideas to other ideas
- will be a letter of introduction to introduce yourself to a great mind
- will be a letter of introduction to introduce one great mind to another

2. Construct imaginary dialogues:

- between yourself and great minds   (example follows)

  You: "Socrates, if you believed so much in the po-tential goodness of humanity and that humans are capable of great things, why were you not more active to end slavery and the subjugation of women in Athens in your day?"

  Socrates: "The mindset of Athens was not ready for many departures from the primitive mentality from which Pericles led us. We simply did not have sufficient perspective upon ourselves to see that Athenian citizenship should include all in our midst, not just those whose power had been traditionally recognized. In spite of our shortcomings, at least we were the first people on earth to witness an aristocracy diminish its power voluntarily and transfer it to the *demos* (people). We made our small contribution to the evolution of thought upon the planet, something your own generation often takes for granted.

- dialogues between two or more great minds (for ex-ample: construct imaginary dialogues between Socrates and Buddha, Emerson and St. Teresa, or Mozart, Einstein, and Aristotle, etc.)

3. Plan a trip to visit a great mind's era:

- describe what you would like to see and do in that era

- describe what you could bring with you as a hospitality gift
- list several questions you would ask the great mind
- list a few items you would bring to inform the great mind about your own era

4. **Prepare a thank you note to a great mind for his or her contributions**

5. **Imagine that a great mind asks your advice and create a response**

6. **Determine what you really want in life, your highest goals and:**

- compare these with what you have discovered as being the goals held by different great minds
- compare strategies for reaching your goals with those of great minds having similar goals
- compare your personal life path with those of great minds
- imagine that particular great minds were offering you advice about your life path

Journal Suggestions to Enhance The ACTIVATORS and Exercises

Many exercises and activities in this book mention recording your own ideas and insights in a journal to stimulate reflection and broaden your understanding of the ideas great minds have produced. For those exercises that do not contain a specific reference to recording your insights in a journal, consider recording your immediate impressions to be an appropriate response whenever you encounter new thoughts or ideas. In addition, record your thoughts *anytime* you use one of the ACTIVATORS to promote enhanced understanding of the idea or insight.

ACTIVATOR: Idea Files — Thomas Edison & Walt Whitman

All ideas are second hand, consciously or unconsciously drawn from a million outside sources and used by the garnerer with pride and satisfaction.

Mark Twain, letter to Helen Keller

Douglas Hofstadter believes that every "new" idea we encounter actually rests upon an unseen foundation of numerous previously discovered ideas. Perhaps that is what Sir Isaac Newton meant when he proclaimed that he was no genius; rather, he was successful simply because he stood on the shoulders of the geniuses who had preceded him. For example, Newton acknowledged that he had combined Kepler's ideas on planetary motion with Galileo's discoveries about the motion of projectiles to form the framework for his own theories about gravity and the Laws Of Thermodynamics. Other highly successful people attribute many of their ideas to earlier discoveries made by others.

One of the great "idea–relaters" was Thomas Edison, perhaps the archetypal inventor. Edison, like other great minds, kept track of good ideas, either his own or those generated by others. He maintained extensive idea files to stimulate new perspectives for his current projects. Edison felt strongly that an idea needs to be original *only in its adaptation to our problem at hand.* A creative mind recognizes, perhaps on an unconscious level as Twain suggests, the essential merits and attributes of a good idea and can adapt these elements to other applications thereby "creating" a new idea. Many of Edison's breakthroughs came from this process.

EDISON'S IDEA FILE

GOAL: To develop a method for adapting ideas to our current needs.

The first step in using Edison's technique is to create your own idea file. Collect any ideas that you feel have potential application to your needs: your study of great minds (e.g., what great minds think about life after death, commonalities among great minds' educational experiences, how great minds felt about their contemporaries, etc.), your practical needs (e.g., innovative personnel management techniques, trends in music composition, special effects photography, novel kitchen designs, etc.), or areas of general interest. You may also include your own ideas in the idea file. Collect any thoughts or ideas which you feel have broad application or strike you as novel or interesting in any way. Be open to your intuitive hunches when collecting ideas!

Record your ideas on notecards and store them in file boxes. In the event you need further information about an idea, indicate the source where you found the idea. Cross reference any ideas that may fit into several different categories. Once you have created an idea file, use the following steps to apply pertinent ideas to your needs.

1. Whenever you experience a problem or need, spend a few minutes listing the situation's essential attributes:

- Its origin or source
- Any obstacles or difficulties you may encounter
- The procedures you already have tried that were either successful or unsuccessful
- How others may be involved with the situation
- Resources involved (people, equipment, supplies, etc.)
- The particular skills that may be needed
- Your intuitive impressions about the situation
- Any other attributes you may feel to be relevant

2. Retrieve any ideas from your file that you feel may apply to your current need. Spread the ideas out before you and review them for a few minutes. Use the following suggestions to select the ideas most suited to your needs:

• Select the ideas containing attributes closely related to any of the attributes form step 1

• Select the ideas generated by people having experience dealing with similar situations

• Select ideas having the most efficient use of resources

• Select ideas you intuitively feel could apply

3. Once you have selected several ideas from the larger group, prepare to apply the ideas to your current needs. You may realize that the entire idea applies or only one procedure or portion of the idea applies. Likewise, ideas may have to be modified in order to apply them to the situation. Use the following suggestions as a guide:

• Apply the one idea that you intuitively feel will work "as is"; it may not be the most logical choice, but it "feels" right to you

• Apply the one idea that you intuitively feel will work with slight modifications

• Combine and apply appropriate attributes or procedures from two or more ideas

• Treat the cause and not the symptoms of the problem; apply the idea most suited to dealing with the source or origin of your problem rather than the effects of the problem

• Apply the idea whose producer has the most experience dealing with similar situations

• Apply each idea and note the effects that each one has upon the problem; select idea offering the best effects

• Apply the one offering minimum waste or maximum resource conservation

• Apply the idea offering other people the opportunity to become involved

4. Once you have addressed the situation, record your observations in your journal and note what you have learned from this activity. Perhaps some of your observations will be candidates for your idea file.

WHITMAN'S IDEA TAPESTRY

GOAL: To create and use relationships among ideas — *an excellent technique for probing secrets from great minds.*

Walt Whitman was another great mind who collected ideas to stimulate his creative potential. His journals describe an ingenious technique he developed for collecting and using in his work any particularly novel ideas he encountered. Anytime an idea would strike his imagination or would demonstrate a relationship to his current creative needs, he would write it down upon a small slip of paper. He placed these slips into various envelopes that he had titled according to the subject area each envelope contained. In order to have a place for each new idea he encountered, Whitman kept ideas in many different envelopes.

Whitman, whenever he felt a need to spawn new thoughts or perspectives, would select the various envelopes pertaining to his current subject or interests. He retrieved ideas from the envelopes, randomly at times or, on other occasions, only those ideas relevant to his subject; then he would "weave" these ideas together as if he were creating an "idea tapestry." These freshly woven relationships often became the foundation for a new poem, essay, or journal entry. Whitman consistently allowed his intuitive nature to guide him as he selected and combined the idea fragments into new relationships.

We can use Whitman's basic technique to create our own idea tapestries from the ideas we encounter, especially the ideas great minds have provided. The following suggestions will help you initiate your personal idea tapestry.

1. Collect ideas that you find interesting or challenging: quotations or ideas from the great minds, unusual terms or phrases you encounter, thoughts from your own journal, miscellaneous odd facts, ideas stimulated by using the ACTIVATORS or other exercises, etc. Write each item on a separate slip of paper.

2. Prepare and title "envelope homes" for the ideas you collect. Each envelope should contain only one subject area (e.g., things great minds said about children, odd characters from literature, ways to show joy, surprising facts about great minds, etc.) Place the slips into envelopes which you feel are most appropriate. As ideas bear relationship with each other, an idea may have several possible "envelope homes." If you feel the idea relates to different subjects, duplicate it and place it into the appropriate envelopes. Once you have developed a fairly extensive idea base, there are several methods to glean insight from your collection.

Exploring ideas from great minds: Gather envelopes containing ideas by or about the great minds. Select, either randomly or by choice, several ideas for the exercise. Perform the following activities to initiate your exploration:

• Select an idea that you wish to explore and find the one you think is most similar — explore the similarities and the possible reasons for them

• Select an idea from a particular great mind and then find all the ideas that express a similar understanding or perspective — explore why these different people have expressed similar ideas

• Select a particular subject you wish to explore (for example, great minds' thoughts about human destiny) and use all the ideas from that envelope; place the ideas in approximate chronological order and review them for a moment—explore the idea's chronological development and the potential implications of this development

- Select an idea and then write your own comment or response to the idea

- Combine two or more ideas, either in whole or in part, to produce a new idea — explore your new creation and its potential applications

- Focus upon a particular problem or need that you have and select ideas that offer assistance — explore these ideas and their application to your needs

- Let your intuition be your guide and create additional activities to explore the ideas

Developing inspiration for writing: If you desire inspiration for creative writing or for your journal, consider using the following activities to stimulate creative thinking:

- Randomly select story elements (plot, theme, characters, setting, etc.) from your idea envelopes containing these subject areas. Create a story from these random elements. For example, you might draw the interesting character you saw last week in the museum, an unusual cathedral for setting, unrequited love for theme, and some recent foreign policy escapade you read about as plot. Playfully combine these elements into a story

- Carefully select story elements to develop a particular theme or idea you have in mind

- Randomly select items from different envelopes — explore in your journal how these diverse ideas may interrelate

- Again, allow your intuition to help you create additional activities that will keep your mind active and stimulated, a requirement for developing our highest mental and spiritual potential

ACTIVATOR: Nuclear Shorthand — Alfred, Lord Tennyson

GOAL: To generate insight from our thoughts and life experiences by encouraging associative thinking –or– to promote mental flexibility by encouraging openness and receptivity to new ideas or experiences.

PREMISES

•*The brain works associatively* — The brain's basic neural structure is designed to create associations among all our thoughts and experiences. The brain's frontal cortex (where our higher thought processes occur) is a vast network comprised of approximately 10 billion neurons or nerve cells. *Each* of these neurons in the cortex may make as many as 10,000 separate connections with other neurons. For all practical purposes, the potential to make neural connections is unlimited.

Each time we process a new idea or experience, we stimulate neural cells in the cortex. Stimulation causes neural cells to form new connections with each other which, in turn, produces a memory item to be stored within the neural network. The brain stores these related memory items along neural pathways, so related items may be recalled together according to their particular associative elements. For example, the various aspects comprising your memory of your first school day — the other students, your teacher, your feelings, what you did, etc. — would be stored together in associative patterns along neural pathways.

Each idea or experience we store contains hundreds, possibly thousands, of potential associations that can combine with each other and enhance our mental potential.

In fact, researchers have established a direct correlation between the ability to form mental associations among these ideas and experiences and our potential to be fully creative.

• *Associative thinking nurtures creative thinking* — Creativity researcher Dr. Sarnoff Mendick maintains in his book, *The Associative Basis of Creativity*, that creative thinking stems from forming new connections among the pre-existing associative elements of our neural pathways. In other words, to enhance our creative potential, we must stimulate the formation of new mental connections among the elements we have already experienced and processed as memory items. Techniques such as **Nuclear Shorthand** can generate new insight from our current knowledge and experience base. It also will stimulate new insights as you read the "Secrets From Great Minds" that follow.

• *Idea generation must be separate from idea evaluation* — Idea generation is an open-ended, associative process that demands receptivity to new combinations of ideas; therefore, we must keep our minds open to new, unusual, or seemingly illogical insights produced during idea generation. Idea evaluation, on the other hand, is a discriminatory, judgmental process that utilizes logical and analytical activities to reach closure on ideas and insights produced by idea generation. Since idea generation and idea evaluation are antithetical activities, they must be kept separate. Switching back and forth between them as we explore an idea or life experience thwarts associative thinking and wastes mental energy. To develop your highest creative potential, remember that idea evaluation must follow idea generation.

BACKGROUND ON NUCLEAR SHORTHAND

Alfred, Lord Tennyson's fellow poet and companion, Arthur Henry Hallam, observed Tennyson closely for many years. Hallam noticed that Tennyson often could reel in the highly elusive ideas which "played tag" in his mind. According to Hallam, Tennyson became quite proficient at retrieving these fragments of thought and used them as a *nucleus* from which his writings would spring. Tennyson would explore these fragments, usually a word or short phrase which popped into his mind, and let them trigger any associated ideas and images connected with the nucleus. This process allowed a stream of ideas to gush forth where only a trickle previously had been found. The Activator, **Nuclear Shorthand**, is based upon Tennyson's discovery of how to generate ideas through associative thinking.

The title comes from the fact that we will use a word or phrase we wish to explore as the "nucleus," and from it associative idea streams will grow like the tributaries of a river. The shorthand aspect stems from the graphic means used to record the flow of ideas so that we are not encumbered by our usual demand for syntax and grammar as we write. Since grammar and syntax are evaluative and judgmental activities, we must avoid them during associative thinking. We also should delay all judgment about the ideas or associations we generate until *after* the idea stream exhausts itself. This enables the mind to stay in the associative, idea–generation mode, and it avoids the frustration and mental exhaustion produced by switching back and forth between idea generation and idea evaluation. The exercise is a powerful technique for either initiating a new idea stream or developing new perspectives on ideas others have already generated.

PROCEDURE

1. Use **Nuclear Shorthand** to explore a idea, word, or phrase that just "pops" into your mind. You may also use it to generate new insight for yourself from ideas others have already produced, such as the wisdom from great minds contained in this book.

2. You will need a clean sheet of paper, preferably one without lines. Write the "nucleus" (the word, phrase, or short synopsis of the idea) in the center of the paper and draw an oval around it. Next, allow any ideas or impressions about this nucleus come into your mind.

Write *whatever* enters your mind, even if it makes little sense or seems inappropriate. Write quickly and do not stop to judge or evaluate any particular item. Write these associations down as if they were branches sprouting from the main word.

3. Draw a circle around each new idea as soon as you have recorded it. The last idea you record becomes the next "nucleus" in the idea stream. Use it to trigger a new association which, in turn, becomes a "nucleus." Draw lines to connect each idea in the stream. You may use a word or phrase more than once during the session.

4. Continue adding new associations to the idea stream flowing from the main nucleus until you feel that it is exhausted. If you need concerted effort to go any further with an idea stream or you stop to judge or evaluate any ideas, you probably have exhausted that stream. Go with your hunches! Through time you will develop an intuitive "feel" for the end of an idea stream.

5. When you feel that you have truly exhausted the flow of potential ideas and associations for the nucleus word, it is time to explore and evaluate your associations. Suggestions to evaluate your associations include:

• Look for words appearing more than once. Their appearance in different idea streams indicates their importance to the main word or idea under investigation.

• Determine which idea stream "feels" most useful or important to you. Taken as a whole, what importance does it have for you? Is it relevant to any situation or problem you now face?

• Notice if your more positive ideas seem to be closer to the nucleus or towards the end of each stream. This may indicate that your nucleus item and its immediate associations are potentially the most meaningful to you and that more remote associations may not hold as much value. Likewise, if you find the more positive items at the ends of idea streams and further away from the nucleus, this may mean you are breaking free of constraints or limits you may ordinarily experience with the nucleus item. Explore what either of these observations could mean to you.

• Are there any items that now produce an immediate emotional response? Explore your response to these items. What does this tell you? Trust your hunches!

• Is there a word or phrase that somehow distinguishes itself from the rest? Perhaps this term deserves to become a nucleus for another session of **Nuclear Shorthand**.

6. Record in your journal any new insights for the nucleus that you have uncovered. Be open to any new perspectives or insights that may surface as you record your ideas. Often, new insights arrive while recording ideas in your journal. If you feel that an idea or insight created through **Nuclear Shorthand** "hits you like the blast of a trumpet" as Emerson says, you may want to include it in your Personal Bible.

ACTIVATOR: The Questioning Techniques — Duchamp & Socrates

GOAL: To encourage natural inquisitiveness which nurtures our creative potential.

Consider these thoughts for a moment:

A question is a midwife to new ideas.

Socrates

I know that curiosity brought me to my best ideas.

Albert Einstein

It is not the answer that enlightens, but the question.

Eugene Ionesco

To wonder is to begin to understand.

José Ortega y Gasset

It is only when we question all our learning that we begin to know.

Henry David Thoreau

It's a healthy idea, now and then, to hang a question mark on things that we have long taken for granted.

Bertrand Russell

Children are innately inquisitive. They riddle their parents and other adults with an endless barrage of questions in order to explore and understand the world around them, even at the risk of asking a "dumb" question every now and then. Children must intuitively realize, as do the great minds quoted above, that learning how to form questions (the *process* of questioning) can be as potentially rewarding as any answers they encounter. Something happens to children as they grow older, however, that diminishes their natural questioning activities and increases their complacency to accept answers furnished by others. That something is school.

Our educational system, with its emphasis upon knowing the "correct" answers to questions, does little to encourage children to explore the *process* of seeking answers or the *process* of forming their own questions. Instead of nurturing our curiosity by encouraging these processes, school, in many ways, actually stifles our innate inquisitiveness. For example, students generally receive praise anytime they provide the teacher with the "correct" answer (the answer the teacher considers appropriate) and criticism anytime their answer differs from the acceptable response. Once students perceive that school rewards those students who know the correct answer, they have learned our educational system's most fundamental lesson: "I **know**; therefore, I am." Innate inquisitiveness yields to the pressure to know the right answers in order to gain acceptance as a person.

Socrates probably would be most alarmed by our modern educational methodology. He, despite being considered by his contemporaries to be the wisest person among them, rarely claimed to "know" much of anything, because he knew that the ability to form questions was as valuable as knowledge itself. His teaching method stimulated pupils' natural inquisitiveness by having them participate in prolonged questioning sessions known as the dialectic method. Socrates realized that teaching people how to form questions, not how to recite approved answers, would free them to search for their own answers and avoid dependency upon whatever answers were currently in vogue.

Socrates shares with many other great minds the understanding that active questioning will help us develop our highest potential by furnishing us with new insights and perspectives about ourselves and the world. Questioning invigorates our minds as we allow new ideas to flow through our mental networks, while unquestioning minds will tend to become stagnant like still ponds. In addition, active questioners, because they take few things for granted, tend to perceive everyday reality as a richer, more fulfilling experience than those whose minds are filled with ready-made answers. Active questioning rekindles our innate inquisitiveness and allows us to develop our highest mental and physical potential, just as it has for many great minds.

RECREATIONAL QUESTIONING — MARCEL DUCHAMP

Many contemporary artists, musicians, and writers maintain that Marcel Duchamp inspired their own thinking through his incessant attempts to unravel the fabric of accepted belief. Duchamp perfected the art of turning traditional or routine thought patterns inside out to expose their weaknesses. Once he had exposed their weaknesses, Duchamp refrained from establishing new thought structures to take their place. Instead, he encouraged people to develop new perspectives for themselves using the same method he had — through recreational, yet purposive, questioning.

Duchamp's ability to become intrigued by even the most mundane elements of life stimulated his playful, inquisitive nature. His imagination could transform commonplace things and events into amusing, yet thought–provoking, questions which kept his mind active. Examples include:

The Physics of Luggage:

What is the difference between the volumes of air displaced in a suitcase by a clean, folded shirt and the same shirt when it is dirty?

The Metaphysics of Death:

Q. At what moment does death occur?

A. The moment you say to yourself, "I've got to settle down in the near future."

Procedure for Recreational Questioning — *Noticing Exceptions*

We, like Duchamp, can train our minds to notice exceptions to our routine or habitual thought patterns (our "conventional wisdom") and use this awareness to enhance our creative potential. Such "exceptions" could occur if you were to notice the effects of a co–worker's novel approach to handling angry clients or to notice how a friend's unusual response to changes in scheduled activities seems to lessen frustration. Anytime you notice an "exception," record your observations in an *Exception Journal.* This journal could be part of your other journals or an entirely separate one. Leave adequate space under each noted exception to make comments and observations. As you explore the wisdom from great minds presented in this book, you may notice "exceptions" to your traditional ideas and beliefs. Record these in your journal.

Occasionally look for patterns among the exceptions you have recorded. Do certain beliefs, thoughts, or actions seem to jump out at you as exceptions, or do you notice exceptions in many diverse life experiences? Consider why you noticed these particular items as exceptions. What possible value or meaning do these exceptions hold for you? If you like, use this awareness to create "recreational questions," questions that incorporate your observations and give new perspective upon things you may have taken for granted. Remember, recreational questioning's primary goal is to stimulate natural inquisitiveness about our life experiences.

THE WEEKLY QUESTIONING SESSION

Another way to encourage natural inquisitiveness is to make it a part of our weekly activity schedule. We accomplish this by setting aside a small amount of time each week to review our prior week's experiences. Once you have reviewed the week's experiences, ask yourself questions to stimulate more thought. A weekly questioning session requires a small time commitment; however, the rewards will be substantial. Regular weekly questioning sessions not only will provide many new insights that have practical applications, but they also will reinforce natural inquisitiveness.

Each weekly questioning session should focus upon our experiences during the previous week. Naturally, if you keep a journal, the session will be more profitable as your thoughts and observations will be more readily available to explore. You may want to use the session to explore the Exception Journal or any other journal you are keeping. Each session requires only about 30 minutes, so it will fit easily into even the busiest schedule. A comfortable place with few distractions will enhance the session. Use the the following suggestions to develop your questioning skills.

1. Find a suitable time for your weekly questioning session. One goal should be to establish a regular time for your sessions. For example: Wednesday evenings at 8:00 P.M. or Saturday mornings at 9:00 A.M. could be your "appointment" with yourself.

2. RELAX! Release thoughts about other activities before you begin the questioning session.

3. Use the questions below as a starter for the questioning session. Try not to force answers; just let them flow naturally into your mind. Focus your full attention upon activities and events of the prior week as you answer the questions. Record your answers in your journal.

THIS PAST WEEK:

• What did I learn from the great minds?

• What great mind(s) had the most influence upon my thoughts? Why?

• How can I apply what I've learned from the great minds this week to my life?

• What feedback could I offer the great minds based upon my experiences this week?

• What exceptions to my habitual patterns of thinking or understanding did I notice?

• What should I do with these exceptions I've noted?

• How did I treat my unconventional or outlandish ideas? Those of other people? What does this tell me?

• What spiritual awareness did I seek? How will this quest benefit me? Benefit others?

4. Once you complete your questioning, contemplate your answers. What have you gleaned from the questioning session? What new insights arrive through exploring your answers? How can you use these insights in the coming week? Are there any thoughts you need to explore further? As you can see, contemplation often means more questioning.

5. Use these new insights. Incorporate them into your mental network and problem-solving repertoire. In future weekly questioning sessions, ask yourself how you have used these insights in your life. Make notes reflecting the insights you have applied, where you applied them, and the outcome of their applications. Use this additional feedback to fine-tune your insights. This reinforces both the initial insight, as well as the active questioning process itself.

How to use this book continued:

4. Practice the Exercises and Techniques

As discussed previously, great minds discovered and utilized many techniques to stimulate their minds and develop their innate potential. If we have similar goals, then we should employ similar methods. This book contains adaptations of more than forty exercises actually used by great minds. Experiment with their techniques as you read the secrets to determine the ones most appropriate to your needs. Practice the techniques regularly, just as the great minds did, and reflect upon the insights they generate in your journal. Consider your efforts to be an investment in yourself!

5. Share — Network — Utilize the Secrets

As you read and explore the secrets from great minds, undoubtedly, several ideas will strike you as being especially important. Using the ACTIVATORS may help integrate these secrets into your life which, in turn, may generate additional insights. In addition to the ACTIVATORS, sharing your insights with friends, relatives, and colleagues and applying the insights to your daily needs are other means to activate your discoveries. Also, consider writing on notecards any quotations from great minds that seem especially meaningful to you. Post the notecards on your desk, bulletin board, refrigerator door, or wherever you will encounter them frequently. You may want to add your comments or observations to the ideas you have posted. Occasionally reflect upon these ideas as you encounter them.

6. Develop Meditative Awareness

Great minds often transferred their awareness from their local mind to their universal mind to receive insight and guidance from this higher source. Most likely, you not only will receive similar guidance, but you also will reduce tension and stress, increase your mental efficiency, and improve your wellness — all of which will give you a high yield on your time investment.

BEGINNING THE EXPERIMENT

Part Two of this book contains twenty one secrets from great minds that exemplify their many discoveries. Spend time with each secret, especially the first four, before you move on to other secrets. Let your intuitive awareness lead you through the secrets and be open to the insights your intuition reveals. If you do not understand an idea, seek assistance from the great minds themselves. Use your imagination and your intellect to speculate what great minds think. Consider, for example, what Aristotle, Einstein, Emerson, or Confucius might think about the idea. Emerson believes that: "All life is an experiment. The more experiments we make, the better!"

It is time to begin this experiment!

PART TWO: THE TWENTY ONE SECRETS

Inspirational Wisdom from the Great Minds

- Why Study Secrets From Great Minds?
- Universal Oneness and Unity
- Nowness and Being
- Intuitive Truth — God — Lies Within
- The Mind Creates Our Reality
- Know Thyself
- Self–acceptance
- True Wealth Lies Within
- Childlike Perception
- The Fountain of Youth Lies Within
- Creative Illumination from the Universal Realm
- Dreams
- Synesthesia
- The Golden Rule
- True Friendship
- Unconditional Love
- Meditation and Contemplation
- Enlightened Vision
- GAIA — Our Earth Mother
- Co–creation
- What Then Must We Do?

WHY STUDY SECRETS FROM GREAT MINDS?

The mission of great minds is to guide humanity over the sea of error into the havens of truth.

Arthur Schopenhauer, *Counsels and Maxims*

Our first secret opens the doorway into all the secrets to follow. It addresses why we should study great minds and the wisdom they have contributed to humanity through the ages. As you explore this secret, focus your attention upon the reasons great minds have advocated that we should study classical thoughts. Also, focus upon how classical wisdom can help you with your life's journey. A number of reasons why we should study these secrets follows below. As you read the comments, add your own observations and reasons for studying secrets from great minds.

We have an innate need to learn

Twentieth–century psychologists Carl Jung, Abraham Maslow, Jean Piaget, Rollo May, Carl Rogers, and many others, concur that one of the most fundamental characteristics of humanity is our innate need to learn, to explore and understand the world around us. Naturally this innate need assisted us in our earliest years as we learned how to function in our environment, and it also facilitated learning during our school years. Our innate need to learn, however, did not diminish when we completed our formal education. Since our need to make sense of the world is both innate and universal among humans, it continues throughout our lifetime. Regretfully, some people abandon or ignore this innate need to learn upon attaining adulthood. They may assume their formal education has suitably prepared them for careers and life experiences so they pay little attention to this fundamental human need. Great minds have always realized that we cannot take the world for granted, nor can we ever stop learning, without harming our human potential. We should study secrets from these great minds to help satisfy our innate desire to learn.

Great minds study other great minds

Aristotle and Plato quoted Homer and Sophocles. St. Thomas Aquinas quoted Aristotle, Plato, and Plotinus. Thoreau quoted St. Thomas, Plotinus, and Buddha. Emerson quoted them all. At one time it was expected that a well–educated person, and most certainly any college graduate, would be well-versed in the classic knowledge generated by great minds such as these. Today, however, colleges seem more intent to prepare students for the career world and not the world of ideas.

Traditional collegiate emphasis upon classical wisdom has been replaced, to a significant degree, with an emphasis upon wisdom of the marketplace and more vocational subjects such as accounting, public relations, advertising, and marketing. Many prominent groups such as the Carnegie Foundation note that the liberal arts are in a widespread decline in the modern age. This is most unfortunate. Great minds have always recognized the value of studying the works of others who are seeking to expand their conception of the universe and to make a contribution to humanity. Sir Isaac Newton, when asked how was it possible for him to have made so many discoveries, replied, "By standing on the shoulders of all the geniuses who came before me." We, too, may obtain Newton's broad perspective as we do what great minds before us have done — study classical wisdom.

East meets West

The current curriculum debate at Stanford and other leading universities posits interesting questions before us regarding the extent that we in Western civilizations need to study Eastern cultures. Those advocating a predominantly Western approach to civilization have taken the perspective that great minds from the East and West are so radically different as to require that they be studied independently of each other — and never the twain shall meet! It is true that, in a narrow, purely academic perspective, there are substantive differences in the ways that Western and Eastern minds have addressed the universe and the human condition within it. Great minds, however, do not have narrow perspectives. They recognize the tremendously valuable contributions made by great minds from other cultures. They have discovered that — at the most fundamental levels — there is more commonality between Eastern and Western thought than many people realize. Stripped of our usual dogma and cultural blinders, East does meet West through great minds.

We can share the inspiration of great minds

"The creative act is not performed by the artist alone," states artist/philosopher Marcel Duchamp. "The spectator brings the work in contact with the external world by deciphering and interpreting its inner qualifications and thus adds contributions to the creative act." From this perspective, we are not merely passive recipients of other people's creations, but are active participants in the creative process itself. If we are to make appropriate contributions to any creative act by our efforts, then we should be fully prepared to accept this responsibility. We start to assume our responsibility by studying great minds to broaden our aesthetical understanding. This provides insight into the inspiration of those who create, whether their creation be written, painted, danced, or in any other possible means of expression. Great minds stand ready to assist our becoming active participants in the creative process, for both our own and humanity's benefit.

Ancient wisdom promotes revelations

As much as we might like to think human understanding has progressed substantially in the several thousand years of civilization, we must accept that, in reality, little has changed. Our most visionary scientists today confirm conceptions of the universe espoused long ago by great minds in many diverse cultures around the world. For example, modern "Quantum Physics" supports the ancient idea that a fundamental oneness and universality pervades the universe, and modern biological science now investigates the venerable "Gaia" hypothesis that our planet itself is actually a biological lifeform like you or I. Today science and ancient spiritual wisdom are merging into a unified explanation of the universe and our place within it. It has taken society as a whole a long time to unite what great minds have long accepted as reality.

Summary

The ideas above are only a few reasons to study secrets from great minds. Other reasons will develop as you explore their works personally and involve your own insight and perspectives in the process. Please use the activities suggested in the *Introduction* to provide invaluable assistance as you read the secrets and attempt to reveal their wisdom. Keep an ongoing journal of your thoughts to provide continuity and enhanced perspective as you read the secrets. In addition, Emerson's **Make Your Own Bible** exercise will promote deeper understanding of the secrets so you can integrate their wisdom into your life. Be patient, and the wisdom from great minds will become available to you.

~~~

Perspectives from Great Minds

~~~

Nature has placed in our minds an insatiable longing to see the truth.

Cicero, *Tusculanes Disputationes*

All people naturally desire knowledge.

Aristotle, *Metaphysics*

The superior person extensively studies literature.

Confucius, *Analects*

Those who influence the thoughts of their own times influence all the times that follow. They make their impress on eternity.

Hypatia

Who is a wise person? One who learns of all people.

Talmud

The life that is unexamined is not worth living.

Plato, *Apology of Socrates*

Rely on the noble,the steady, the learned, the prudent, the wise. One wise enough to follow such beings is like the path of the stars.

Buddha, *Dhammapada*

Oh may I join the choir invisible of those immortal dead who live again in the minds of those made better by their presence.

George Eliot, "Oh May I Join..."

Every day that we spend without learning something is a day lost.

Beethoven

If your daily life seems poor, do not blame it; blame yourself, tell yourself that you are not poet enough to call forth its riches.

Rainer M. Rilke, *Letters to a Young Poet*

The only means of strengthening one's intellect is to make up one's mind about nothing — to let the mind be a thoroughfare for all, thoughts.

John Keats, *Letters (Sept. 17, 1819)*

Nobody, I think, ought to read poetry or look at paintings or statues who cannot find a great deal more in them than the poet or artist has actually expressed.

Nathaniel Hawthorne, *The Marble Fawn*

The more we know about the ancients, the more we find that they are like the moderns.

Henry David Thoreau, *Journals*

Living is thinking. It is the occupation of the gods says Aristotle, from which springs their happiness and ours... It is good to rub and polish your mind against the minds of others.

Montaigne, *Essays*

Thought once awakened does not again slumber.

Thomas Carlyle, *Heroes and Hero-worship*

The human mind, once stretched to include a single new idea, does not shrink back to its original proportions.

Oliver Wendell Holmes

Nurture your minds with great thoughts.

Benjamin Disraeli

To know that which before us lies in daily life is the prime wisdom.

John Milton, *Paradise Lost*

For every nation, there are messengers.

Koran

Nothing is so productive of elevation of the mind as to be able to examine methodically and truly every object which is presented to you in life, and always to look at things so as to see what kind of universe this is.

Marcus Aurelius, *Meditations*

The real advantage which truth has consists in this, that when an opinion is true, it may be extinguished once, twice, or many times, but in the course of the ages there will generally be found persons to rediscover it, until some one of its reappearances falls on a time when by favorable circumstances it escapes persecution until it has made such headway as to withstand all such subsequent attempts to suppress it.

John Stuart Mill, *On Liberty*

Everyone is a creature of the age in which they live; very few are able to raise themselves above the ideas of the times.

Voltaire, *Essay on the Morals and the Spirit of Nations*

To be learning something is the greatest of pleasures not only to the philosopher, but also to the rest of humanity.

Aristotle, *Poetics*

Study the teachings of the Great Sages of all sects impartially.

Gampopa, *Rosary of Precious Gems*

There are always in the world a few inspired people... who spring up.

Plato, *Laws*

Those who develop their minds to the utmost can serve Heaven and fulfill their own destinies.

Mencius

From the beginning of the world there have always been God-enlightened people.

The Sophic Hydrolith

Like the bee gathering honey from different flowers, the wise person accepts the essence of different scriptures and will see the good in all religions.

Srimad Bhagavatam

If we reach the heart of our own religion, we also reach the heart of other religions.

Gandhi

As soon as the mind is sufficiently developed, there awakes in us the spiritual preoccupation, the discovery of a self and inmost truth and beauty, and the release of our mind and life into the truth of the Spirit, its perfection by the power of the Spirit, the solidarity, unity, and mutuality of all beings in the Spirit.

Sri Aurobindo, *The Life Divine*

UNIVERSAL ONENESS AND UNITY

The sage grasps the universe by the arm. He blends everything into a harmonious whole.

Chuang Tzu

Throughout history, scientists and mystics have sought the secrets of the universe through divergent means. Scientists have explored the physical universe with the best "tools" available to them at any given time. The primary tools ancient scientists used to explore the universe were their unaided senses. Even though they could not reach to the heights or depths of the universe that modern science now attains, they discovered a fundamental wholeness and unity everywhere the human eye or ear could turn.

For twentieth–century scientific explorers, however, electron microscopes, radio telescopes, atom smashers, and particle accelerators are the best tools available. Modern scientists, just like their predecessors, have found that whether we extend the eyes and penetrate inside the atom, or whether we penetrate to the furthest reaches of the heavens, we will find wholeness and unity at every level. Twentieth–century "quantum physics" has found wholeness and oneness at both the subatomic and galactic realms, just as did many scientists using their unaided senses in the "see–touch" realm of earlier days.

Mystics, on the other hand, always have searched for universal wisdom within themselves. Their primary tools have been meditation, and contemplative prayer. Mystics, in spite of using radically different methods from the scientists, also discovered that all things are one, that all things are part of a universal "Essence." The inner voyages of the mystics, therefore, tends to corroborate the external investigation of the scientists.

Today, whether our focus be upon the physical world around us or upon the spiritual domain within us, we, too, can discover the oneness and unity permeating the entire universe. If you seek this wisdom for yourself, perhaps the following ideas will be a starting place for this quest.

~~~~~~

Perspectives from Great Minds

~~~~~~

Astonishing! Everything is intelligent!

Pythagoras

The essence of humanity is to comprehend a whole; or that which in the diversity of sensations can be comprised under a rational unity.

Plato

How all things weave themselves into the whole, one working and living into the other...all sounding harmoniously through the All.

Goethe, *Faust*

In things spiritual there is no partition, no number, no individuals. How sweet is the oneness — unearth the treasure of Unity.

Rumi, *Masnavi*

The cosmos is one living organism.

Plotinus, *Enneads*

Never see anything without seeing God therein.

Sufi Proverb

Frequently consider the connection of all things in the universe and their relation to one another.

Marcus Aurelius, *Meditations*

Quantum physics forces us to see the universe as...a complicated web of interrelationships between the various parts of a unified whole....The basic oneness of the universe becomes apparent at the atomic level and manifests itself more and more as one penetrates deeper into the realm of subatomic particles.

Fritjof Capra, *The Tao of Physics*

Energy is the only life — the Body and Reason is the bound or outward circumference of Energy.

William Blake, *Marriage of Heaven and Hell*

A human being is part of the whole called by us "Universe." We experience ourselves, our thoughts and feelings as something separated from the rest — a kind of optical delusion of consciousness. This delusion is a prison for us. Our task must be to free ourselves from this prison by widening our circle of compassion to embrace all living creatures and the whole of nature.

Albert Einstein, *Ideas and Opinions*

All are but parts of one stupendous whole,
Whose body is Nature, and God the soul.

Alexander Pope, *Essay on Man*

Those who regard all things as one are companions of nature.

Chuang Tzu

One who loves God finds the object of his love everywhere.

Sri Aurobindo, *The Life Divine*

The universe is as inseparable from the universal mind as a man's ideas are inseparable from his own mind...When we know fully by insight the essence of the tiniest ant, we know also the essence of the whole universe.

Paul Brunton, *The Wisdom of The Overself*

All things are implicated with one another, and the bond is holy...for there is one universe made up of all things, and one God who pervades all things.

Marcus Aurelius, *Meditations*

Whatever you perceive by fleshly sense you perceive in part, not knowing the whole of which those things are but parts.

St. Augustine, *Confessions*

Inconceivable as it seems to ordinary reason, this life of yours is not merely a piece of the entire existence but is, in a certain sense, the whole.

Erwin Schrödinger, *My View of the World*

The disciple must know God as the One who eternally becomes the Many, the Many who in their apparent division are eternally one.

Sri Aurobindo, *Essays on the Gita*

It is true that the Godhead is Three, but the Three is again comprised in the One...And because God transforms himself into the One, we on Earth must also strive for the One...and live in it.

Paracelsus

Each being contains in itself the whole intelligible world. Therefore, All is everywhere. Each is All and All is each.

Plotinus, *Enneads*

Just as God is one simple thing in existence in every way but is multiple in conceptuality, so too the universe is one thing but is multiple in parts and distinct things.

Meister Eckhart, *Commentary on the Book of Wisdom*

There is only one wisdom: to recognize the intelligence who steers all things.

Heraclitus, *Fragments*

I am what is around me.

Wallace Stevens, *Collected Poems*

The one infinitely variable Spirit in things carries all of itself into each form of its omnipresence...God moves in many ways at once in this indivisible unity.

Sri Aurobindo, *The Problem of Rebirth*

When you are identified with the One, all things will be complete to you.

Chuang Tzu, *The Record*

God is one and therefore likes unity.

Mohammed, *The Hadith*

Thou art All and All is in Thee.

The Apocrypha, Acts of Peter

Whence shall he have grief, how shall he be deluded, the one who sees everywhere the Oneness.

Isha Upanishad

The whole contains nothing that is not for its advantage. By remembering that I am part of such a whole, I shall be content with everything that happens.

Marcus Aurelius, *Meditations*

Identification with the All leads to supreme Allness. Study to attain the condition of this Allness.

Aparokshanubhuti

For those who see Me everywhere and see everything in Me, I am never lost, nor are they ever lost to Me.

Bhagavadgita

Each object in the world is not merely itself but involves every other object, and in fact *is* in every other object.

Hindu Sutra

Everything leads us to believe that there is a certain point in the spirit from which life and death, real and imaginary, past and future, communicable and incommunicable, are no longer perceived as contraries.

André Breton, *Second Manifesto*

From the revolution of the world to our own breathing, there is nothing that is not K'ai-ho (unity of coherence).

Shên Tsung-ch'ien

There is something undifferentiated and yet complete which existed before heaven and earth.

Lao Tzu, *Tao Tê Ching*

Think of It, speak of It, enlighten one another in It; this is full devotion to the idea of Oneness.

Panchadasi Upanishad

The infinite mind of the All is the womb of the cosmos.

The Kybalion

There is one mind common to all individual men ...One who has access to this universal mind is a party to all that is or can be done.

Ralph Waldo Emerson, *"History"*

A grain of sand includes the universe.

Samuel Taylor Coleridge, *"Thought"*

Though earth and man were gone,
And suns and universes ceased to be,
And Thou wert left alone,
Every existence would exist in Thee.

Emily Brontë, *"Last Lines"*

The hidden harmony is better than the obvious.

Heraclitus, *Fragments*

Unity cannot be numbered itself. It creates innumerable kinds from itself and contains them all within itself.

Macrobius, *Commentary on the Dream of Scipio*

There is one common flow, one common breathing: *all things are in sympathy.*

Hippocrates

Every atom belonging to me as good belongs to you.

Walt Whitman, *Song of Myself*

Every form of life, every form of consciousness is conditioned and depends on the totality of all that exists or ever came into existence. The more that we become conscious of this infinite interrelationship, the freer we become because we liberate ourselves from the illusion of separation.

Lama Govinda, *Creative Meditation
and Multi-Dimensional Consciousness*

NOWNESS & BEING

The creative person, in the inspirational phase of the creative furor, loses his past and his future and lives only in the moment. He is all there, totally immersed, fascinated and absorbed in the present.

Abraham Maslow, *The Further Reaches of Human Nature*

When the cavalier European adventurers sailed the Atlantic and landed in what they considered to be a new world, they encountered many astonishing realities that shook the foundations of their rather narrow mindset. One of their most perplexing discoveries was the native peoples of the Americas whose intimate spiritual relationship with the world around them confounded the dogmatic religious tenets of the European conquerors. Almost without exception, the natives existed outside measured time, *in the now*. So predominant was their focus upon the now, upon the universe just as it is, that they had little capacity in their languages even to express past or future realities.

Their spiritual awareness was nurtured by seeing the world as a continuous flowing of events, much like the flowing of a stream, without needing to segregate any particular event as a static, isolated happening that has come and gone. They also spent little time thinking about the future, for they knew that "living in the now" is the most propitious way to create a meaningful future. The secret these people possessed is one of the secrets shared by great minds. The native people of the Americas, like the great minds, dwell in a universe outside ordinary human concepts of time — in the eternal, infinite *NOW*.

Perspectives from Great Minds

As if you could kill time without injuring eternity.... God culminates in the present moment, and will never be more divine in the lapses of all the ages.

Henry David Thoreau, *Walden*

The present is a powerful deity.

Goethe, *Torquato Tasso, Act IV*

Forget the passage of time... Relax in the realm of the infinite and thus abide in the realm of the infinite.

Chuang Tzu

When our soul sheds light to us we are in the present — infinite, and not in the past or the future which are both finite, willed into existence.

Ralph Waldo Emerson, "The Over-Soul"

All those happenings a billion years ago,
Are happening now, all around us: time.
Indeed this morning the little sparrow hopped about
In that nebulous whirlpool
A million light years hence.

Shinkichi Takahashi, "The Position of the Sparrow"

The Present is all thou hast
for thy sure possessing;
Like the patriarch's angel,
hold it fast 'till it gives its blessing.

John Greenleaf Whittier, "My Soul and I"

This present moment is all we have... the "when" of the future or the "then" of the past always involves an artificiality, a separating one's self from reality.

Rollo May, *Man's Search for Himself*

In the eternal, nothing but the whole is present...and all flows out of that which is ever present.

St. Augustine, *Confessions*

In rivers, the water you touch is the last of what has passed and the first of that which is to come: so with the time present.

Leonardo da Vinci

We cannot lose either the past or the future: for what we do not have, how can anyone take this from us?... For the present is the only thing of which we can be deprived.

Marcus Aurelius, *Meditations*

The soul that ascends to worship God is plain and true; it dwells in the hour that now is, by reason of the present moment.

Ralph Waldo Emerson, "The Over-Soul"

We must not wish for anything other than that which happens from moment to moment.

St. Catherine of Genoa

We should be blessed if we lived in the present always.

Henry David Thoreau, *Walden*

Real generosity towards the future lies in giving all to the present.

Albert Camus, *The Rebel*

Make use of time, let not advantage slip;
Beauty within itself should not be wasted:
Fair flowers that are not gathered in their prime,
Rot and consume themselves in little time.

Shakespeare, "Venus and Adonis"

I am in the present.... That is what I am called upon to serve, and I serve it in all humility.

Igor Stravinsky, *An Autobiography*

The sufi is the child of the time present.

Rumi, *Masnavi*

Relate not with the future, nor with what has gone by; live the present out with a smiling heart.

Yogavasishtha

Confine yourself to the present.

Marcus Aurelius, *Meditations*

The surest way to create something is losing oneself in the present...being inspired by the surroundings...yielding to what is directly before us.

Vincent van Gogh, *The Letters of van Gogh*

Whenever a mind is simple and receives a divine wisdom, it lives now and absorbs past and future into the present hour.

Ralph Waldo Emerson, "Self-Reliance"

There is no past or future in art. If a work of art cannot always live in the present, it must not be considered art at all.

Pablo Picasso, "Statement, 1923"

No longer forward nor behind I look in fear;
But grateful, take the good I find, the best of now and here.

John Greenleaf Whittier

Past and future veil God from our sight; burn up both of them with fire. How long will you be partitioned by these segments?

Rumi, *Masnavi*

Now is the watchword of the wise.

Lao Tzu, *Tao Tê Ching*

They that have time, and look for a better time, will lose time.

Oh, seize the instant time; you will never power the mill with waters that have already passed by.

Sufi Proverbs

Who with clear vision can see,
The present which is here and now:
Such wise one should aspire to win,
What never can be lost or shaken.

Buddha, *Pali Canon*

I live in the present. I only remember the past and anticipate the future.

Henry David Thoreau, *Letters*

In the moment of our talking, envious time has ebbed away,
Seize the present, trust tomorrow as little as you may.

Horace, *Epistles*

Take no thought of the morrow, for the morrow shall take thought for the things of itself.

Jesus of Nazareth

Those who postpone the hour of living as they ought are like the fool who waits for the river to pass before crossing; the river glides on, and will glide on forever.

Horace, *Epistles*

This hour's the very crisis of your fate,
Your good and ill, your infamy or fame,
And the whole color of your life depends
On this important now.
    John Dryden, "The Spanish Friar"

The roses under my window make no reference to former
roses or to better ones; they are for what they are. There is
no time to them...but humans postpone and remember. We
cannot be happy and strong until we too live with nature in
the present above time.
    Ralph Waldo Emerson, *Journals*

When the mind leaves behind its dark forest of delusion, you
will go beyond times past and times still to come.
    Bhagavadgita

One ought apparently to live in the continuous present.
    George Orwell

To Be is to live with God.
    Ralph Waldo Emerson, *Journals*

In time there is no present,
In eternity no future,
In eternity no past.
    Alfred, Lord Tennyson, "The How and the Why"

Everything for today, nothing for yesterday, nothing for
tomorrow.
    Francis Picabia, in *Artists on Art*

One main characteristic of the peak experience is just a total
fascination with the matter at hand, getting lost in the
present.
    Abraham Maslow, *The Further Reaches of Human Nature*

For the creation of a master-work of literature, two powers must concur, the power of the author and the power of the moment.

Matthew Arnold, "The Function of Criticism"

There is neither time nor space, neither before nor after, but everything present in one new, fresh-springing *now* where millenniums last no longer than the twinkling of an eye.

Meister Eckhart, *Sermons and Collations*

A preoccupation with the future not only prevents us from seeing the present as it is, but often prompts us to rearrange the past.

Eric Hoffer, The Passionate State of Mind

"I AM WHO I AM."
Exodus 3:14

When you stop talking to yourself and are simply aware of what is, that is to say what you feel, what you sense... you suddenly find that the past and the future have completely disappeared.

Alan Watts, *OM, Creative Meditations*

The future you will know it when it has come; before then, forget it.

Aeschylus, *Agamemnon*

The person least dependent upon the morrow goes to meet the morrow most cheerfully.

Epicurus

Do not occupy your time except with the most precious of things, and the most precious of human things is the state of being occupied between the past and the future.

Ahmad 'Isa al-Kharraz

THE TRUTH — *GOD* — LIES WITHIN

The highest revelation is that God is in everyone.

Ralph Waldo Emerson, *Journals*

One of the most consistent secrets shared by great minds — both past and present, and Eastern and Western — is that the universal truth known as God lies within each of us. Great spiritual teachers Buddha, Jesus, and Mohammed concur with great philosophers Plato, Plotinus, Seneca, and Voltaire. Great Western writers Ovid, Blake, Wordsworth, and Emerson concur with the writers of Eastern texts such as the Hindu *Kathopanishad*, *Bhagavadgita*, and *Sutralamkara*. Once we survey the messages from these and other great minds, there can be little doubt concerning the divine presence that dwells in each of us.

Unfortunately, several modern religious ideologies downplay our resident divinity and place far greater emphasis upon pointing out human shortcomings and our isolation from God due to the doctrine of original sin. The true message of the great spiritual leaders has been narrowed down by the over-emphasis upon sin so that, instead of seeing God's presence within us and using it to guide us, many people mistakenly assume that we are unworthy of God's omnipresence, oneness, universality, and love.

Granted, each of us may fall far short of our true potential as part of the divine plan; however, we never fall outside God's presence, nor does God abandon us or desert the dwelling place created within us. If we desire to find our true relationship with the Divine Essence, then we must begin our search with the answers already residing within us. That is where great minds initiated their relationship with God, and it must be our starting place as well. The great minds offer us their insights as signposts for our journey within.

Perspectives from Great Minds

One has to realize the truth within oneself.

Sutralamkara

Truth is within ourselves;
it takes no rise from outward things,
whate'er you may believe.
There is an inmost centre in us all,
Where truth abides in fullness.

Robert Browning, *Paracelsus*

Your own heart is the dwelling place of the Essence of the
Universe.

Sufi Master Attar

Behold, Thou dost desire truth in the innermost being,
And in the hidden part Thou wilt make me know wisdom.

Psalm 51:6

There is an eye of the soul which...is far more precious than
ten thousand bodily eyes, for by it alone do we see truth.

Plato, *Republic*

The seed of God is in us. Pear seeds grow into pear trees,
nut seeds into nut trees, and God seeds into God.

Meister Eckhart, *Sermons*

We possess in ourselves the Illuminating Intellect, a spiritual
sun ceaselessly radiating, which activates everything in
intelligence, and whose light causes all our ideas to arise in
us and whose energy permeates every operation of our
mind. This primal source of light cannot be seen by us; it
remains concealed in the unconscious.

St. Thomas Aquinas, *Summa Theologica*

We must bring the vision within and no longer see in the mode of separation. We need no longer look outside for our vision of the divine being; it is but the strength to see divinity within.

Plotinus, *On Intellectual Beauty*

Peace comes when our souls realize that ...at the center of the Universe dwells the Great Spirit, and that this center is really everywhere, it is within each of us.

Black Elk, Lakota Sioux Elder

He who knows his own self knows God.

Mohammed, *The Hadith*

The nature of the Living Being outside me I can understand only through the Living Being which is within me.

Albert Schweitzer, *Out of My Life and Thought*

God is in your heart, yet you search for God in the wilderness.

The Granth, a Sikh Text

If anyone is bewildered, it is only because they do not see the creator, the holy Lord abiding within themselves.

Maitrayana-Brahmana Upanishad

If God is not within us, then God never existed.

Voltaire, *La Loi Naturelle*

As fragrance dwells in a flower, and reflection in a mirror,
So does God dwell in every soul, seek God therefore in thyself.

Sikh Master Nanak

Highly ought we to rejoice that God dwells in our soul, and much more highly ought we rejoice that our soul dwells in God.

St. Julian of Norwich, *Revelations of Divine Love*

When you have shut the doors and made a darkness within, remember never to say that you are alone, for God is within.

Epictetus, *Golden Sayings*

The Lord abides in the heart of all things.

Bhagavadgita

Nothing is void of God: God fills all creation.

Seneca, *De Beneficiis*

All perfection of which the outer man is capable is only a realization of the eternal perfection of the Spirit within himself.

Sri Aurobindo, *The Synthesis of Yoga*

Abandon the search for God...Learn who it is within you... To know the Self is to know God.

Gnostic Gospels from the Nag Hammadi Library

I believe that God is within me just as the sun is in the color and fragrance of a flower; the Light in my darkness, the Voice in my silence.

Helen Keller

The kingdom of God is within you.

Jesus, *Luke 17:21*

God in us worships God.

Ralph Waldo Emerson, *Journals*

Only those who see God in themselves find eternal peace.

Kathopanishad

The life force is in everything, the life force is manifested on all planes.

Seventh Hermetic Principle

There is a divinity within our breasts.

Ovid, *Epistulae ex Ponto*

The universe is the outward visible expression of the Truth within us, and the Truth is the inner unseen reality of the universe around us.

Jami, *"Lawa'ih"*

It is with the interior eye that truth is seen.

St. Augustine

Find Buddha in your own heart.

Zen Master Eisai

God can be known only by God.

Theologia Germanica

God enters by a private door into every individual.

Ralph Waldo Emerson, *"Intellect"*

THE MIND CREATES OUR REALITY

All we are is the result of what we have thought; we are made by our thoughts.

Buddha, Dhammapada

In Ursula LeGuin's novel, *The Lathe of Heaven*, the main character discovers that anything he dreams about somehow becomes reality, not only for himself, but for other people as well. If he dreams about wanting it to stop raining, it stops raining. This plot may seem far-fetched; however, it may prod us into the awareness that, in many ways, both our conscious and unconscious thoughts actually do become our reality. Great minds long ago discovered that whatever we *choose* to be our thoughts will influence both our perception of reality and our responses to those perceptions to such an extent that our thoughts actually create our physical and spiritual realities.

So extensively can our thoughts influence physical reality that scientists are establishing the connection between our thoughts and our physical health. Recent medical studies clearly link our thoughts with an increased vulnerability to cancer, heart disease, diabetes, and other diseases. In fact, researchers indicate that as much as 80% of all illness can be traced to the harmful effects that stress has upon our immune system. The evidence makes it clear: stressful thoughts will create an unhealthy reality.

What is true on the physical level is also true on the spiritual. The thoughts we have about our soul and its relationship with the universal soul will influence our spiritual reality. Thoughts that nurture a spiritual awareness and presence in our lives actually will create that reality for us.

Likewise, negative, self–centered thoughts will denigrate our spiritual reality and separate us from the universal soul.

The remarkable thing is that we always have a choice about what will become our thoughts. No one can force us to think about anything against our will. Perhaps we should *choose* our thoughts more carefully, just as many great minds have done, because our thoughts are destined to become our reality.

Perspectives from Great Minds

Being and thought are one.

Obituary of Jean Dubuffet

They can do all things because they think they can.

Virgil, *Aeneid*

If anyone is unhappy, let them remember that they are unhappy by reason of themselves alone.

Epictetus, *Golden Sayings*

The tongues of wise people are in accord with their minds.

Egyptian Book of Ptat-Hotep

The actuality of thought is life.

Aristotle, *Metaphysics*

Those who form desires in their minds become offspring of those desires.

Mundaka Upanishad

All that we are is the result of what we have thought; it is founded on our thoughts, it is made of our thoughts.

Buddha, *Dhammapada*

Heavy thoughts bring on physical maladies; when the soul is oppressed, so is the body.

Martin Luther, *Table-Talk*

You conquer fate by thought.

Henry David Thoreau, *Journals*

Our life is what our thoughts make it.

Marcus Aurelius, *Meditations*

So long as a man imagines that he cannot do this or that... so long it is impossible to him that should do it.

Spinoza, *Ethics*

As we think in our hearts, so we are.

Proverbs 23:7

What one does and what one thinks, that is what he becomes.

Brhadaranyakopanishad

Believe that your life is worth living and your belief will help create the fact.

William James, *The Will to Believe*

The transmigration of one's life takes place in one's mind. Therefore keep the mind pure, for what we think, that we become.

The Upanishads

To think is first of all to create a world (or to limit one's own world which comes to the same thing).

Albert Camus, *The Myth of Sisyphus*

We are what we believe.

Anton Chekhov, *Notebooks*

The world is nothing but mind. All is mind.

Lankavatura Sutra

Take away the complaint, "I have been harmed," and the harm is taken away.

Marcus Aurelius, *Meditations*

Both heaven and hell come from one's own mind.

Sayings from the Kurozumi Kyo

The mind is its own place, and in itself
Can make a heaven of Hell and a hell of Heaven.

John Milton, *Paradise Lost*

You give birth to that on which you fix your mind.

Antoine de Saint-Exupéry, *Lifestream*

Each of us literally chooses by his way of attending to things what sort of universe he shall appear to himself to inhabit.

William James, *Principles of Psychology*

It is the mind that makes the person.

Ovid, *Metamorphoses*

You are what you love.

St Augustine

God gave man speech, and speech created thought, which is the measure of the universe.

Percy Bysshe Shelley, *Prometheus Unbound*

If you are pained by any external thing, it is not this that disturbs you, but your own judgment about it. And it is in your power to wipe out this judgment.

Marcus Aurelius, *Meditations*

It is the mind that maketh good or ill,
That maketh wretch or happy, rich or poor.

Edmund Spencer, *The Faerie Queen*

There is nothing either good or bad, but thinking makes it so.

Shakespeare, *Hamlet*

It is the mind which gives to things their quality, their foundation, and their being. Whoever speaks or acts with impure mind, him sorrow follows.

Buddha, *Dhammapada*

The world is just your thought.

Maitri Upanishad

Since it always happens that one gives form and substance to dangers upon which one broods to excess, the dread of the possibility becomes an accurate forecast of the future.

George Sand, *Story of My Life*

Change your awareness, and you live in a different world, you experience a different reality.

Lama Govinda, *Creative Meditations and Multi-Dimensional Consciousness*

KNOW THYSELF

One who knows others is wise.
One who knows himself is enlightened.

Lao Tzu, *Tao Tê Ching*

Plato writes that one of Socrates' strongest beliefs was that self–knowledge is essential to developing both our mental and spiritual potential. The renowned oracle at Delphi attested to Socrates' belief as the inscription over the portal through which all seekers of wisdom passed had but one requirement for entry, KNOW THYSELF. Indeed, how could anyone solicit wisdom from the oracle or any external source without awareness of the wisdom that already lies within.

Self–knowledge gives us sufficient perspective on our lives so that we more easily identify any rationalization, fear, or motive that might be counterproductive to either our own interest or the interests of others. Without the enhanced perspective obtained through self–knowledge, we may reject or downplay not only our own intuitive wisdom, but also wisdom from external sources. Throughout history, many great minds have harvested the benefits gleaned from their self–knowledge and have woven this wisdom into the overall pattern of their creative endeavors.

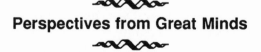

Perspectives from Great Minds

Self-knowledge is the shortest road to God.

Sufi Master 'Azîz ibn Muhammad al-Nasafî

Socrates: "I must know myself, as the Delphian inscription says; to be curious of that which is not my concern, while I am still in ignorance of my own self, would be ridiculous."

Plato, *Phaedrus*

Koyla: "It is my opinion that the trouble in the world comes from people who do not know who they are."

Lillian Hellman, *North Star*

Thoroughly to know oneself, is above all art, for it is the highest art. If you know yourself well, you are better and more praiseworthy before God.

Theologia Germanica

Any technique which will increase self-knowledge in depth should in principle increase one's creativity.

Abraham Maslow, *The Further Reaches of Human Nature*

Whosoever would attain to the summit of his noble nature and to the vision of the sovereign good, which is God, must have the profoundest knowledge of himself.

Meister Eckhart

Whoever knows himself well knows his Maker.

'Alî, *Maxims*

One who reflects upon himself, reflects upon his own original.

Plotinus, *Enneads*

One knowing his nature, also knows heaven.

Mencius, *The Works of Mencius*

If I am not I, who will be?

Henry David Thoreau, *Journals*

You know Me in you, and from this knowledge you will derive all that is necessary.

St. Catherine of Siena, *Dialogue*

No one can be saved without self-knowledge.

St. Bernard, *Sermon XXXVII*

If you do not know yourself...go follow after the steps of the flocks.

Canticle of Canticles

When you wake up, you will find that this whole world, above and below, is nothing other than a regarding of oneself.

Hakuin, *The Embossed Tea Kettle and Other Works*

We never come to full knowing of God till we know first our own soul. For until the time that our soul has its full powers, we cannot be fully holy.

St. Julian of Norwich, *Revelations of Divine Love*

Let us enter the cell of self-knowledge.

St. Catherine

The inquiry, "Who am I? " is the only method to put and end to all misery and usher in supreme Beatitude.

Sri Ramana Maharshi, *Self Inquiry*

Whoever knows the All but fails to know himself lacks everything.

Jesus in *The Gospel According to Saint Thomas*

You ought, O Soul, to get sure knowledge of your own being...all things that you ought to get knowledge of are in your possession and within you.

Hermes, *De Castogaione Animae*

Let me know myself, Lord, and I will know Thee.

St. Augustine, *Soliloquies*

One who knows not who he is and to what end he was born...is not this ignorance the cause of all human mistakes and mischances?

Epictetus, *Golden Sayings*

The individual who wishes to have an answer to the problem of evil, as it is posed today, has need, first and foremost of self knowledge.

Carl Gustav Jung, *Memories, Dreams, Reflections*

Self-knowledge, our human realization of the Divine, is the Self in us becoming all existences.

Sri Aurobindo, *The Life Divine*

Take care about this: however sublime the contemplation, let your prayer always begin and end with self-knowledge.

St. Teresa of Avila, *The Way of Perfection*

I turn my gaze inwards, I fix it there and keep it busy...I continually observe myself, I take stock of myself, I taste myself.

Montaigne, *Essays*

SELF–ACCEPTANCE

Healthy individuals find it possible to accept themselves and their own nature without chagrin or complaint. They can accept their own human nature with all its discrepancies from the ideal image without any real concern.

Abraham Maslow, *Motivation and Personality*

Few people have made more significant contributions to the concept of self–acceptance than has Henry David Thoreau. "As I regard myself, so I am" is but one of his many commentaries about the importance of self–acceptance for those on a journey towards self–realization. Thoreau confirms the wisdom shared by other great minds that our self–acceptance actually determines who we are and who we can become. Self–acceptance means that we fully accept our humanness—our ability to make both wise choices and mistakes—without affecting our value as a human being.

As we are children of God, the Universal Creative Essence, we have within us a portion of that divinity. To the extent that we lack self–acceptance, we deny or denigrate the divinity that has been placed within us. To the extent that we can separate our self–worth from our actions and behaviors and place it where it belongs—upon our inherent value as children of the Divine—we move towards self–actualization, towards realizing our full mental and spiritual potential. Fortunately, we can turn to the great minds for guidance with this task.

Perspectives from Great Minds

As for conforming outwardly, and living your own life inwardly, I do not think much of that.

Henry David Thoreau, *Letters*

Popular opinion is the greatest lie in the world.

Thomas Carlyle, *"Goethe"*

Above all, thine own self respect.

Pythagoras, *The Golden Verses*

The good man does not grieve that others do not recognize his merits.

Confucius, *Analects*

Socrates: "Acquit me, or do not acquit me; but be sure that I shall not alter my way of life, no, not if I have to die for it many times."

Plato, *Apology of Socrates*

A happy life is one in accordance with its own nature.

Seneca

Juliet: "'Tis but thy name that is my enemy.
      Thou art thyself though, not a Montague."

Shakespeare, *Romeo and Juliet*

No one can make you feel inferior without your consent.

Eleanor Roosevelt, *This is My Story*

When someone asked da Vinci what was his greatest accomplishment he replied, "Leonardo da Vinci."

The greatest thing in the world is for a man to know how to be himself.

Montaigne, *Essays*

I want to show others a man just as he is, true to his nature; and this man will be myself. I am not made like any of those I have come across. If I am not better, at least I am different.

Rousseau, *Confessions*

Whatever crushes our individuality is despotism.

John Stuart Mill, *On Liberty*

Public opinion is a weak tyrant compared with private opinion. What I think of myself, that determines my fate.

Henry David Thoreau, *Journals*

My life is for itself and not for a spectacle. What I must do is all that concerns me, not what people think. Trust thyself... great people always do.

Ralph Waldo Emerson, *"Self–Reliance"*

I exist as I am, that is enough,
If no other in the world be aware I sit content,
And if each and all be aware I sit content.

Walt Whitman, *Leaves of Grass*

In knowing ourselves to be unique, we possess the capacity for becoming conscious of the infinite. But only then!

Carl Gustav Jung, *Memories, Dreams, Reflections*

I celebrate myself and sing myself.

Walt Whitman, *Song of Myself*

Whoso would be a person must be a nonconformist.... nothing is at last sacred but the integrity of your own mind.

Ralph Waldo Emerson, *"Self–Reliance"*

Self–love is the instrument of our preservation; it is necessary.

Voltaire, *Philosophical Dictionary*

If our true inner nature is permitted to guide our life, we grow healthy, fruitful and happy.

Abraham Maslow, *Toward a Psychology of Being*

A man knows when he has found his vocation when he stops thinking about how to live and begins to live.

Thomas Merton, *Thoughts in Solitude*

One must not respect the opinion of another more than one's own...One must respect one's own opinion most.

Democritus, *Canons*

To be nobody–but–myself in a world which is doing its best, night and day, to make you into everybody else... means to fight the hardest battle which any human being can fight and never stop fighting.

e. e. cummings, *Letters 1955*

I would prefer to be known as I really am, even with all my faults, than as someone with imaginary virtues who is not me.

Rousseau, *Confessions*

If a man does not keep pace with his companions, perhaps it is because he hears a different drummer. Let him step to the music which he hears, however measured or far away.

Henry David Thoreau, *Walden*

TRUE WEALTH LIES WITHIN

Superfluous wealth can buy superfluities only. Money is not required to buy one necessity of the soul.

Henry David Thoreau, *Walden*

Western culture abounds with myths and legends concerning the acquisition of wealth. The pot of gold at the end of a rainbow, Rumpelstiltskin spinning straw into gold, King Midas' touch, and Horatio Alger stories are but a few of the myths about wealth passed down from one generation to the next. These and similar stories maintain that wealth is something to be pursued out in the world. This perspective also implies that we are in direct competition with each other for finite, worldly riches. Since our material resources are limited and competition for them is most keen, we cannot increase our own material wealth without causing others to suffer loss. Rumpelstiltskin, after all, did demand quite an exorbitant price for his magic.

Imagine for a moment that, instead of perpetuating these myths about wealth, we taught our children that true wealth is not outside us, but is found inside us—*within our soul*. No longer would we have to be in competition with each other for wealth, since our inner wealth is unlimited and vastly more satisfying than finite, material wealth. We also could shift our attention away from materialistic preoccupations and focus it more upon development of the soul. We would become more like the great minds who, in spite of hearing the prevailing myths about wealth, always have known that true wealth lies within.

Perspectives from Great Minds

One who is plenteously provided for from within, needs but little from without.

Goethe, *Maxims, Volume V*

I hold that to need nothing is divine, and the less a man needs, the nearer does he approach divinity.

Socrates, quoted by Xenophon

It is not the possessor of many things whom you can rightly call happy.

Horace, *Odes*

The path that leads to worldly gain is one thing, the path to nirvana is quite another.

Buddha, *Dhammapada*

That one who is exceptionally good should also be exceptionally wealthy is a mere impossibility.

Plato, *Laws*

The wealth of the soul is the only true wealth.

Lucian, *Dialogues*

If the darkness caused by material entanglements has been removed from the eyes of your soul, then you will see the blessed vision radiating in the pure heaven of your soul.

St. Gregory of Nyssa, *Sermon Six on the Beatitudes*

Do not weary yourself to gain wealth, cease from consideration of it.

Proverbs: 23:4

The "unreality" of material things is only relative to the greater reality of spiritual things...We cannot see things in perspective until we cease to hug them to our bosom. Only then can we see God in them.

Thomas Merton, *Thoughts in Solitude*

Do not lay up for yourselves treasures upon earth where moth and rust destroy and where thieves break through and steal. But lay up for yourself treasures in heaven where neither moth nor rust destroys and where thieves do not break through and steal; for where your treasure is, there will your heart be also.

Jesus in Matthew 6:19-21

The truly pure of heart are those who despise the things of earth and seek the things of Heaven.

St. Francis of Assisi, *Admonitions*

A free life cannot acquire many possessions.

Epicurus, *Fragments*

The more a man lays stress upon false possessions, and the less sensitivity he has for what is essential, the less satisfying is his life. He feels limited because he has limited aims.

Carl Gustav Jung, *Memories, Dreams, Reflections*

The world will trouble you so long as any part of you belongs to the world. It is only if you belong entirely to the Divine that you can become free.

Sri Aurobindo, *Basis of Yoga*

When one follows the way of the world, or the way of the flesh — knowledge of Reality will not arise within him.

Shankara, *The Crown Jewel of Wisdom*

Love of money is the birth of all ills.

Diogenes

An enlightened person should endeavor only for the minimum necessities of life.

Srimad Bhagavatam

A man is rich in proportion to the number of things he can afford to let alone.

Henry David Thoreau, *Walden*

This is what you should do: love the earth and sun and animals, despise riches, give alms to everyone that asks, and devote your income and labor to others... and your very flesh shall become a great poem.

Walt Whitman, *Preface to Leaves of Grass*

Socrates: "Take no thought for your persons and your properties, but first and chiefly care about the greatest improvement of the soul."

Plato, *Apology*

Of great riches there is no real use. The ways to enrich are many, and most of them are foul.

Francis Bacon, *Essays*

Fear of death increases in exact proportion to increases in wealth.

Ernest Hemingway, *Essay, Law of the Dynamics of Dying*

No person has a right to be respected for any possessions but those of virtue and talents. Titles are tinsel, power a corrupter, and excessive wealth a libel on its owner.

Percy Bysshe Shelley, *A Declaration of Rights*

I am absolutely convinced that no wealth in the world can help humanity forward, even in the hands of the most devoted worker in this cause. Money only appeals to selfishness and irresistibly invites abuse. Can anyone imagine Moses, Jesus, or Gandhi armed with the money-bags of Carnegie?

Albert Einstein, *Ideas and Opinions*

On no particular matter is the public mind more unhealthy than the appetite for money...For it we work and toil, and sweat away our youth and adulthood, giving up our improvement of the mind.

Walt Whitman, *Essay: "Morbid Appetite for Money"*

The enjoyments born of contact between the senses and their objects are, indeed, sources of misery.

Bhagavadgita

The small mind lives in the world of his ephemeral wants and desires, while the great mind lives in the infinity of the universe.

Lama Govinda, *Creative Meditation and Multi-Dimensional Consciousness*

Morals today are corrupted by our worship of riches.

Cicero, *De Officiis*

The greatest wealth is to live content with little, for there is never want where the mind is satisfied.

Lucretius, *De Rerum Natura*

The knower of the Essence, enjoying the pleasures of the senses in moderation, but knowing them for what they are, may derive both temporal as well as spiritual pleasure.

Panchadasi Upanishad

Wealth does not consist of having great possessions, but of having few desires.

Epicurus, *Fragments*

The senses are endowed with a tendency to objectivize; it is hence that they cater to objects without and not the the subject within.

Kathopanishad

Riches do not come from an abundance of goods but from a contented mind.

Mohammed, *The Hadith*

A mind absorbed in sense objects is the cause of bondage, and a mind detached from sense objects is the cause of liberation.

Vishnu Purana

To the extent that a person can...turn away from material things, he will find his unity and blessing in that little spark in the soul.

Meister Eckhart, *Sermons and Collations*

When the heart weeps for things that are lost, the spirit laughs for what it has found.

Sufi Proverb

The superior person thinks of virtue,
The inferior person thinks of possessions.

Confucius, *Analects*

One who chooses the advantages of the soul, chooses things divine. One who chooses those of the body, chooses things human.

Democritus, *Canons*

How can there be any question of acquiring possessions when the one thing needful for a man is to *become*, to *be*.

Antoine de Saint-Exupéry, *The Wisdom of the Sands*

Possessions give me no more than I have already...But in thought, *in my thought*, I comprehend the universe.

Blaise Pascal, *Pensées*

Who is rich? One who is content.

Benjamin Franklin, *Poor Richard's Almanac*

Not to yield to material things is called perfection.

Confucius, *Analects*

If we place our value in outward things — we must then be subject to hindrance and restraint; we become the slave of those who hold power over the things we desire.

Epictetus, *Golden Sayings*

Socrates: "Why do you who are a citizen of the great and mighty and wise city of Athens care so much about laying up the greatest amount of money and honor and reputation, and so little about the greatest improvement of the soul which you never regard or heed at all?"

Plato, *Apology of Socrates*

There is no wealth but life.

John Ruskin, *Unto This Last*

Embrace simplicity,
Reduce selfishness,
Have few desires.

Lao Tzu, *Tao Tê Ching*

A CHILDLIKE NATURE

A childlike adult is not one whose development has been arrested; on the contrary, he is an adult who has given himself a chance of continuing to develop long after most people have muffled themselves in the cocoon of middle age habit and convention.

Aldous Huxley, *Music at Night*

"Genius is nothing more than childhood recovered at will," maintains French poet Charles Baudelaire. Children, whose imagination, playfulness, and curiosity are not shackled by the demands and limitations of adult's logical–rational reality, remain more open to the universe and its inexhaustible supply of mysteries. Their present–tense awareness and preoccupation with natural wonders provide an inexhaustible supply of building blocks for their minds to transform into original and imaginative expressions of joy.

As we mature into adults, however, we tend to replace these innate means of discovery with the "practical knowledge" which will be useful to us in our daily lives. We abandon our active exploration of the world in favor of exerting mastery over it. But, as Baudelaire and numerous other great minds attest, the child remains within each of us. In order to activate our innate creative potential, we simply need to recover our childlike nature at will just as great minds have done.

Perspectives from Great Minds

The great man is one who does not lose his childlike nature.

Mencius, *Book of Mencius*

All my life through, the new sights of nature made me rejoice like a child.

Marie Curie

A first encounter with any new phenomenon exercises immediately an impression upon the soul. This is the experience of a child discovering the world, to whom every object is new.

Wassily Kandinsky, *Concerning the Spiritual in Art*

The sage sees and hears no more than an infant sees and hears.

Lao Tzu, *Tao Tê Ching*

Sit down before a fact like a little child, be prepared to give up every preconceived notion...or you shall learn nothing.

Thomas Huxley, *Letter to Charles Kingsley*

To be surprised, to wonder, is to begin to understand.

José Ortega y Gasset

It has taken me all my like to see again as a child.

Pablo Picasso

Accommodating oneself to the unusual reopens for adults the mysterious kingdom inhabited by children.

André Breton, *Humors*

Knowledge does not consist in accumulation of facts, but in the ever-present faculty of discernment and clear insight into the nature of things. This is possible only if we look at things with fresh eyes—as if we had never seen them before.

Lama Govinda, *Creative Meditation and Multi-Dimensional Consciousness*

Primary creativeness is very probably a heritage of every human being.... Certainly it is found in all healthy children... it is lost by most people as they grow up.

Abraham Maslow, *The Further Reaches of Human Nature*

The voyage of discovery consists not in charting new landscapes, but in having new eyes.

Marcel Proust

Dare to be naïve.

Buckminster Fuller, *Synergetics*

Genius is nothing more nor less than childhood recovered at will—a childhood now equipped for self expression with an adult's capacities.

Charles Baudelaire, *The Painter of Modern Life*

Jesus: "Truly, I say to you, unless you are converted and become like children, you shall not enter the kingdom of heaven."

Matthew 18:3

I don't know what I may seem to the world. But as to myself, I seem to have been only like a boy playing on the seashore and diverting myself now and then.

Sir Isaac Newton

Playfulness is an attitude of mind; play is a passing outward manifestation of this attitude.

John Dewey, *How We Think*

The wolf shall dwell with the lamb, and the leopard shall lie down with the goat; and the calf and the young lion and the fatling together; and a little child shall lead them.

Isaiah 11:6

The greatest poem ever known
is one all poets have outgrown,
The poetry, innate, untold
of being only four years old.

Christopher Morley

All children are born a genius, they just get de-geniused quickly.

Buckminster Fuller

One who approaches persons or paintings or poetry without the youthful ambition to learn a new "language" and so gain access to someone else's perspective on life, let them beware!

Dag Hammarskjöld, *Markings*

Trailing clouds of glory do we come from God,
who is our home:
Heaven lies about us in our infancy...
At length the man perceives it die away,
And fade into the light of common day.

William Wordsworth, *Ode: Intimations of Immortality*

THE FOUNTAIN OF YOUTH LIES WITHIN

Death is a fact that you can do nothing about. Nothing at all. But youth is a quality, and if you have it, you never lose it.

Frank Lloyd Wright

Ponce de León wantonly blazed a path across what he considered to be a new world in a desperate attempt to locate the legendary Fountain of Youth. De León, like others who have sought various materialistic means to conquer the world, depended upon some earthly, external power for assistance and not upon the unlimited power source that resides within each of us. Great minds through the ages have discovered that the true "Fountain of Youth" lies within. Through their relationship with the universe around them, and by devotion to their particular calling to express their visions of the universe, they achieved what de León sought in vain.

Many great minds have expressed that they received an actual physical rejuvenation produced by their dedication to *life as a journey*. Their commitment to developing their highest potential allowed them to be productive long past the demise of many of their less–inspired colleagues. They not only acquired physical well-being from devotion to their lifework, but many also expressed spiritual rejuvenation produced by listening to their inner spiritual reality. Their discovery now stands confirmed by modern researchers who have documented the longevity generated by people who dedicate themselves to experiencing life as a journey towards self–realization. These great minds know that *youth is a state of mind.*

Perspectives from Great Minds

Some thoughts always find us young and keep us so. Such a thought is the love of universal and eternal beauty.

Ralph Waldo Emerson, *"The Over-Soul"*

When we are old, we must do more than when we were young.

Goethe, *Maxims, Vol III*

There is nothing more notable about Socrates than that he found time, when he was an old man, to learn music and dancing, and he thought it time well spent.

Montaigne, *Essays*

To retire is to begin to die.

Pablo Casals (said at age 96)

Within I do not find wrinkles and a used heart, but unspent youth.

Ralph Waldo Emerson, *Journals* (at age 62)

Our life should be so active and progressive as to be a journey.

Henry Thoreau, *Journals*

One's life has value so long as it attributes value to the life of others.

Simone de Beauvoir, *The Coming of Age*

"I am still learning."

Michelangelo's lifelong motto

'Tis very certain the very desire of life prolongs it.

George Gordon, Lord Byron, *Don Juan*

I could not, at any age, be content to take my place in a corner by the fireside and simply look on. Life was meant to be lived. Curiosity must be kept alive!

Eleanor Roosevelt, *NY Herald Tribune, 1961*

Life, if you know how to live it, is long enough.

Seneca, *"On the Shortness of Life"*

For as I admire a young man who has something of the old man in him, so do I admire an old one who has something of a young man. The man who aims at this may possibly become old in body — in mind, he never will.

Cicero, *"Old Age"*

The one with little understanding grows old like an ox. He may put on flesh, but his wisdom never increases.

Buddha, *Dhammapada*

My heart leaps up when I behold
A rainbow in the sky.
So it was when my life began;
So it is now I am a man;
So be it when I shall grow old,
Or let me die!

William Wordsworth, *"My Heart Leaps Up When I Behold"*

Anyone who has a *why* to live can bear almost any *what*..

Nietzsche

When you cease to make a contribution, you begin to die.

Eleanor Roosevelt, *Letters: The Years Alone*

Cato: "I am in my eighty-fourth year...as you see, old age has not quite enfeebled me or broken me down...our minds are rendered more buoyant by exercise."

Cicero, *"Cato Major"*

Old places and old persons in their turn, when spirit dwells in them, have an intrinsic vitality of which youth is incapable; precisely the balance and wisdom that comes from long perspectives and broad foundations.

George Santayana, *My Host the World*

One who has existed only, not lived, lacks wisdom in old age.

Publilius Syrus, *Moral Sayings*

The only thing that makes anybody older is that they cannot be surprised.

Gertrude Stein, *Everybody's Autobiography*

There is only one solution if old age is not to be an absurd parody of our former life, and that is to go on pursuing ends that give our existence a meaning—devotion to individuals, to groups or causes.

Simone de Beauvoir, *The Coming of Age*

CREATIVE ILLUMINATION FROM THE UNIVERSAL REALM

Beneath the real world there is an ideal world, visible in all its splendor to those who have grown accustomed to perceive in things more than just *things*.

Victor Hugo, *Odes et Ballades*

"Talent is that which is in a man's power; genius is that in whose power a man is," proclaims poet James Russell Lowell, delineating one of the most fundamental debates about the origin of creative inspiration—*talent versus genius*. Through the ages humanity has produced a plethora of artistic, scientific, musical, and literary creations. Some of these creations have endured through the centuries and attest to the universal ideas expressed therein. Other creations, even if they were well received in their own times, went to the grave with their producers.

One only has to think of the contrast between the *genius* of Mozart and the *talent* of his disconsolate contemporary, Antonio Salieri, as illustrated in the recent play and movie, *Amadeus*, to understand the distinction. Mozart spoke an eternal musical language, while Salieri spoke only to his own era. But, what is the source of the creative genius for great minds such as Mozart? Thomas Carlyle expresses his conviction that "Genius is the clearer presence of God in man." By no means is he alone in this belief. Great minds consistently have recognized that their role is primarily to be the receiver of creative inspiration, not its source. The true source of creative inspiration is universal, not local, consciousness. If we desire to develop our creative potential, then we, like the great minds, must cultivate universal consciousness.

Perspectives from Great Minds

WRITERS

The unconscious is ever the act of God...The central fact is the super–human intelligence, pouring into us from the unknown fountain, to be received with religious awe and defended from any mixture of our will.

Ralph Waldo Emerson, *Introduction to Essays and Journals*

The poem "Milton" was written from immediate dictation... I dare not pretend to be any other than the secretary; the authors are in Eternity.

William Blake, *Letter to Thomas Butts, 1803*

The description of a character in the epic poem *Hyperion* came by chance or magic...to be, as it were, something given to me.

John Keats, *Letters*

There is a god within us;
we are in touch with heaven:
from celestial places comes our inspiration.

Ovid, *Ars Amatoria*

I know this; the writer who possesses the creative gift owns something of which he is not always master — something that at times strangely wills and works for itself.

Charlotte Brontë, *Preface to Emily's Wurthering Heights*

We are aware of evanescent visitations of thoughts and feelings, the interpenetration of a diviner nature than our own.

Percy Bysshe Shelley, *A Defence of Poetry*

A poet is someone of an extraordinary sensitive and active subconscious personality fed by and feeding a nonresident consciousness.

Amy Lowell

I wrote the book, *Werther*, almost unconsciously, like a somnambulist, and was amazed when I realized what I had done.

Goethe

The poet sometimes seems to have a chamber in his brain into which an angel flies with divine messages.

Ralph Waldo Emerson, *Journals*

The other world is all my art; my pencils describe no other.

Henry Thoreau quoted by Emerson in his essay, *"Thoreau"*

One power alone makes a poet — Divine Vision.

William Blake

I have to suspend my will so my mind becomes automatic and a possible vehicle for spiritual beings.

William Butler Yeats, *A Vision*

No one was ever great without divine inspiration.

Cicero, *De Natura Deorum*

Socrates: "I have had this from my childhood; it is a sort of voice that comes to me."

Plato, *Apology of Socrates*

There is a power above and behind us and we are the channel of its communication.

Ralph Waldo Emerson, *Introduction to Essays and Journals*

All who have achieved real excellence in any art possess one thing in common; that is, to be one with Nature.

Basho

There is another Self; my own personality is but a mere instrument through this spirit is working.

George Eliot

One who in his mind never travelled to Heaven is no artist.

William Blake

I have always written very quickly in some way subject to a rhythm that was seeking through me its living form. Many of my "New Poems" have more or less written themselves.

Rainer Maria Rilke

I desire to spend my life conversing with my friends in Eternity, seeing visions, dreaming dreams and prophesy.

William Blake, *Letter to Thomas Butts, 1803*

I will work out the divinity that is busy within my mind and tend the means that are mine.

Pindar, *Odes*

Suddenly, in some fortunate moment, the voice of eternal wisdom reaches me, even in the strain of the sparrow, and liberates me; whets and clarifies my senses.

Henry David Thoreau, *Journals*

There is a hidden sanity which still guides the poet in his wildest aberrations.

Charles Lamb, *Sanity of True Genius*

I have learned that when your inner helper is in charge, do not try to think consciously. Drift — wait — and obey.

Rudyard Kipling

Enlighten me, O Muses,
tenants of Olympian homes,
For you are goddesses,
inside on everything,
and know everything,
But we mortals hear only the news,
  and know nothing at all.

Homer, Iliad

Socrates: "Not by wisdom do poets write poetry, but by a sort of genius and inspiration; they are like diviners or soothsayers."

Plato, Apology of Socrates

A poet participates in the eternal, the infinite and the one through his partial apprehension of the agencies of the invisible world.

Percy Bysshe Shelley, A Defence of Poetry

Writing poetry is a spiritual activity which makes one completely forget, for the time being, that one has a body.

Stephen Spender, The Making of a Poem

The poet makes himself a seer through a long, prodigious, and rational disordering of all the senses.

Arthur Rimbaud, Preface to Illuminations

Underneath the region of argument and discourse lies the region of meditation; here...dwells the vital force that is in us; here, if anything is to be created, and not merely manufactured, must the work be done.

Thomas Carlyle, Characteristics

The major poetic idea in the world is and always has been the idea of God.

Wallace Stevens, Letters

ARTISTS

The people who weep before my pictures are having the same religious experience I had when I painted them.

Mark Rothko

How I paint I do not know myself... I find in my work an echo of what struck me. I see that nature has told me something, has spoken to me.

Vincent van Gogh, *Letters*

Art does not reproduce the visible; rather, it makes visible.

Paul Klee, *The Inward Vision*

Universal consciousness, intuition, that is, is the origin of all art.

Piet Mondrian, *Natural Reality and Abstract Reality*

My hand is entirely the tool of a distant will.

Paul Klee, *The Diaries of Paul Klee*

My art is a kind of spiritual revelation... synonymous with eternal truth.

Wassily Kandinsky, *Concerning the Spiritual in Art*

I have terrible lucidity at moments when nature is so beautiful; I am not conscious of myself anymore, and the pictures come to me as in a dream.

Vincent van Gogh, *Letters*

A work of art is the product of calculations that are frequently unknown to the artist — calculations that precede intelligence.

Pablo Picasso

COMPOSERS

I have to be in a semi–trance conditions to get results — a condition when the conscious mind is in temporary abeyance...I feel the vibrations that thrill all of me...the spirit illuminating the soul power within me...I realize that I and God are one.

Johannes Brahms

Whence and how my ideas come, I know not; nor can I force them. They take place as if in a pleasingly lively dream. I pray to God and the composition begins.

Wolfgang Amadeus Mozart

The germ of a future composition comes suddenly and unexpectedly — it takes root with extraordinary force and rapidity; frequently in a somnambulist state.

Peter Ilych Tchaikovsky

I did see all Heaven before me and the great God. Wither I was in my body or out of my body as I wrote the "Messiah," I know not. God knows.

George Handel

From where do I get my ideas? That I cannot with certainty say. They come uncalled, directly and indirectly.

Ludwig van Beethoven

The music of *Madam Butterfly* was dictated to me by God; I was merely instrumental in putting it on paper and communicating it to the public.

Puccini

We composers are projectors of the infinite into the finite.

Edvard Grieg

I want to show people how to talk with God.

Leos Janacek

In writing "Electra" and "Rosenkavalier" I was dictated to by Omnipotent entities; by more than an earthly Power. I know that I can appropriate it, and that this holds true for any line of human endeavor.

Richard Strauss

I owe my life work to angelic intelligences and those invisible helpers whom I try to follow.

Alan Hovhaness

Appropriation of one's own soul–forces is the supreme secret...This opens the door for vibration to pass from the dynamo which is the soulcenter, into my consciousness, and the inspired ideas are born.

Puccini

DREAMS

It is in our dreams that the submerged truth sometimes comes to the top.

Virginia Woolf, *A Room of One's Own*

In ancient Greece, people revered their dreams so highly that they often took long journeys to one of the approximately four hundred oracles dedicated to Asclepius, the god of sleep. At these remote sanctuaries scattered throughout the countryside, sojourners would engage in preparatory activities and prayers designed to incubate special dreams that would provide insight into their problems. Incubated dreams were a form of revelation to the ancient Greeks who trusted their dreams just as they would have trusted wisdom from Plato, Pythagoras, or Aristotle.

The Greeks were not alone in their respect for dreams. The Egyptian, Chinese, Hebrew, Mayan, Hindu, Assyrian, and numerous other ancient cultures incorporated the special wisdom found only in the dream state into their daily activities. Likewise, great minds have drawn profound wisdom, artistic inspiration, and even foundations for major scientific breakthroughs from their dreams. Learning to respect the dream state is the first step towards understanding the dream as being an oracle for our own lives.

Perspectives from Great Minds

Hear now my words: If there is a prophet among you, I, the Lord, shall speak to him in a dream.

Numbers 12: 6

I owe real knowledge to dreams...the soul in dreams has a subtle synthetic power which it will not exert under the sharp eyes of day.

Ralph Waldo Emerson, *Journals*

My gracious god, stand by my side. My friendly god will listen to me; God Mamu of my dreams, My god send me a favorable messenger.

Assyrian clay tablet (7th century BC)

In dreams we never deceive ourselves, nor are we deceived... In dreams we act out a part which we must have learned and rehearsed in our waking hours...Our truest life is when we are awake in our dreams.

Henry David Thoreau, *The Week, Wednesday*

The dream is a little hidden door in the innermost and most secret recesses of the psyche, opening into the cosmic night which was psyche long before there was any ego-consciousness.

Carl Gustav Jung, *Collected Works*

Socrates: "In my life I have often had intimations in dreams...the same dream came to me sometimes in one form, and sometimes in another."

Plato's *Phaedo*

Unbroken supreme awareness even in a dream is the mark of the highest order of sages.

Tripura Upanishad

Eyes illuminate the sleeping dream, but in the daylight man's future cannot be seen.

Aeschylus, *Eumenides*

Our dreams are a second life.

Gérard de Nerval, *Aurelia*

It is the right of the painter to excite the imagination and to consider dreams, as well as still life, as material for their art.

Paul Klee

Socrates: "I have been commanded by God through oracles and dreams."

Plato, *Apology of Socrates*

Judge your natural character by what you do in your dreams.

Ralph Waldo Emerson, *Journals*

Dreams are the interpreter of our inclinations.

Montaigne, *Essays*

The dream consciousness seems to be wholly devoid of that control which the waking consciousness exercises to a certain extent over life circumstances.

Sri Aurobindo, *The Life Divine*

Our heart oft times wakes when we sleep, and God can speak to that, either by words, by proverbs, or by signs as well as if one were awake.

John Bunyan, *Pilgrim's Progress*

An unexamined dream is like an unopened letter.

Talmud

When deep sleep falls upon men and they sleep in their beds, then God opens the ears of men and gives them instruction.

Job 33: 15-16

A dream is more precise than a vision and may explain what is obscure in a vision.

Zohar

In our dreams we may even interpret our dreams.

Chuang Tzu

On whatever subject we have much dwelt,…during sleep we pursue our tasks and investigate the nature of things.

Lucretius, *The Nature of Things*

It is even possible to become wholly conscious in sleep and follow throughout from beginning to end or over large stretches the stages of our dream-experience.

Sri Aurobindo, *The Life Divine*

I do not know if I was then a man dreaming I was a butterfly, or if I am now a butterfly dreaming I am a man.

Chuang Tzu

SYNESTHESIA

If the doors of perception were cleansed,
everything would appear to man as it is, infinite.
For man has closed himself up, till he sees all things
through narrow chinks of his cavern.

William Blake

Blake regrets that humanity seems to dwell inside a cave with each of our five senses walled off and isolated from the others to the extent that we lose the contextual reality of our environment. Sensory impressions reach our brain as a holistic reflection of reality. Then, our logical mind categorizes and departmentalizes the unified, holistic sensory experience into discrete, manageable parts. We reinforce this response each time we focus upon one particular sensory impression and pay little attention to the others. For example, when eating a banana we tend to focus more attention upon the taste than the texture, smell, sound, etc., even though all five senses actually are being stimulated. Thus, one level of Blake's comment addresses how we generally lose the contextual reality of sensory experiences.

Another level deals with synesthesia or sensory crossover. Synesthesia occurs whenever one sensory stimulus triggers another sensory response. If a sunset ever whispered to you, if rain ever felt blue as it hit your skin, if an orchestra ever smelled like a rose to you, then, most likely, you have experienced synesthesia. Most adults, however, do not report synesthetic awareness, because adult minds tend to isolate and categorize sensory impressions as Blake noted. Synesthesia seems to be most prevalent among young children and, as you will discover from their comments, among great minds.

Perspectives from Great Minds

Do not deceive yourself; do not think that you "receive" painting by the eyes alone. No, unknown to you, you receive it by your five senses.

Wassily Kandinsky, *"Concrete Art"*

Are my eyes but fools for my other senses?

Shakespeare, *Macbeth*

The sound of your voice is sweet like the full taste of dark wine.

Egyptian Hieroglyph circa 1300 BC

Sensus communis: a common sense that integrates the activity of all the other more specialized senses.

Aristotle, *De anima and De sensu*

A studious blind man bragged one day that he now understood what "scarlet" signified. Upon which his friend demanded to know what scarlet was like since he was blind. The blind man answered that is is like the sound of the trumpet.

John Locke, *An Essay on Human Understanding*

In color there is harmony, melody, counterpoint.

Charles Baudelaire, *"Salon 1846"*

Eyes and ears act with that unison of sense which marries sweet sound with the grace of form.

John Keats, *"Hyperion"*

From arrangements of pebbles, from angled forms, from cracks or holes, from cut out leaves, from colors, from odors and sounds I saw harmonies emerge that were previously unknown....Everything lives, everything acts, everything corresponds.

Gérard de Nerval, *"Aurelia"*

Odor, sight, hearing, and touch participate equally...sounds cloak them selves in colors and colors contain music.

Charles Baudelaire, *"Les Paradis Artificiels"*

When sound and colour and form are in a musical relation, a beautiful relation to one another, they become one sound, one colour, one form and evoke an emotion that is made out of their distinct evocations and is yet one emotion.

W.B. Yeats, *"The Symbolism of Poetry"*

Like music, art acts upon the soul through the intermediary of the senses; harmonies of color corresponding to the harmonies of sound.

Paul Gauguin, *Letters*

This is a delicious evening when the whole body is one sense, and imbibes delight through every pore.

Henry David Thoreau, *Walden*

Mind set free in the Dharma-realm,
I sit at the moon-filled window
Watching the mountains with my ears,
Hearing the stream with open eyes.

Zen Master Shutaku

I truly no longer knew if I breathed music or if I heard perfumes or if I slept among the stars.

Guy de Maupassant, *"La vie errante"*

The high rate of vibration which yields a sharp note to the ear should involve somewhat the same feeling that is produced by the high rate of vibration which, to the eye, yields a violet color. These affinities…should be improved by training.

George Santayana, *The Sense of Beauty*

From the warm conclave of that fluted note
Somewhat, half song, half odor did float,
As if a rose might somehow be a throat.

Sidney Lanier, *"The Symphony"*

The murmur of the gray twilight.

Edgar Allan Poe, *"Al Aaraaf"*

Color is a power which directly influences the soul. Color is the keyboard, the eyes are the hammers, the soul is the piano with many strings.

Wassily Kandinsky, *Concerning the Spiritual in Art*

THE GOLDEN RULE

Surely it is the maxim of loving-kindness: Do not unto others what you would not have them do unto you.

Confucius, *Analects*

The Golden Rule, for most people, is one of the many expressions memorized during childhood as part of our schooling or religious upbringing. We probably were taught that "Do unto others as you would have them do unto you" is the proper way to conduct our relations with others. We also learned that following the Golden Rule would help us become a good citizen and a responsible member of society.

Most likely, we were not taught that this principle lies at the heart of the world's most prominent religions and has served as a guiding influence for great minds throughout the ages. Today, with situational ethics and "the ends justify the means" mentality guiding virtually all powerful and influential people, perhaps we need to rediscover the timeless wisdom of this simple, yet prudent axiom.

Perspectives from Great Minds

All things whatsoever you would have that men should do to you, do so to them.

Matthew 7:12

Do not that to your neighbor that you would not suffer from him.

Pittacus of Lesbos

Desire nothing for yourself which you do not desire for others.

Spinoza, *Ethica*

The duty of man...is plain and simple, and consists of but two points: his duty to God, and with respect to neighbors, to do as he would be done by.

Thomas Paine, *The Rights of Man*

Treat your inferiors as you would be treated by your betters.

Seneca, *Epistolae ad Lucilium*

Be just and gracious unto me, as I am confident and kind to thee.

Shakespeare, *Titus Andronicus*

Hurt not others in ways that you yourself would not find hurtful.

Udana-Varga

Whatsoever you require that others do to you, that do ye to them.

Thomas Hobbes, *Leviathan*

Whatever Christians do not wish to be done to them, they must not do to another.

St. Aristrides, *Apology for the Christian Faith*

Morality: walking like others upon the path.

Chuang Tzu

This is the sum of all true righteousness: deal with others as you yourself would be dealt.

The Mahabharata

What you would avoid suffering yourself, seek not to impose on others.

Epictetus, *Encheiridion*

Every man takes care that his neighbor does not cheat him. But a day comes when he begins to care that he does not cheat his neighbor. Then all goes well.

Ralph Waldo Emerson, *"Conduct of Life: Worship"*

That behavior alone is good which refrains from doing unto another what is not good for itself.

The Dadistan-i-dinik

We should behave to friends as we would wish friends to behave to us.

Aristotle

No one of you is a believer until you desire for others that which you desire for yourselves.

Sunnah

Regard your neighbor's gain as your own gain, and your neighbor's loss as your own loss.

T'ai Shang Kan Ying P'ien

What is bad to you, do not to others. That is the entire Law; all the rest is commentary.

Talmud

Do not to others what would anger you if it be done to you by others.

Isocrates

To do as one would be done by, and to love one's neighbor as one's self, constitute the ideal perfection of utilitarian morality.

John Stuart Mill, *Utilitarianism*

TRUE FRIENDSHIP

Our friend must be broad. His must be an atmosphere coextensive with the universe, in which we can expand and breathe.

Henry Thoreau, *Journals*

Emerson, through his essay "Friendship" which is replete with nuances of his friendship with Thoreau, discusses the various aspects of "true friendship." Emerson presents many factors that contribute to such a relationship, as well as the benefits of having such a relationship. He then synthesizes these ideas into two essential requirements for true friendship. They are:

TRUTH — friends must avoid deception and dishonesty with each other, even when it would be more comfortable for both people if a deception had been created

TENDERNESS — friends must not only be honest and truthful with one another, but they also must share their emotional sensitivities with each other; friends must be genuine human beings in the truest sense of the term

Emerson's essay portrayed friendship to be more than simple caring and respect for another person, more than just enjoying another person's company, or even more than having feelings of affection for another person. *Friendship is life itself*, life expressed in its richest, most fully realized dimension.

A true friend is someone with whom you can discard your rationalizations and pretenses so that you can develop your unique human potential without fear. A true friend is someone whose soul joins with yours in exploration of the universe and with whom you rejoice in your mutual discoveries. Thoreau found in this essay not only a description of his friendship with Emerson, but also the archetypal friendship described throughout human history such as the friendship between Socrates and Plato or Damon and Pythias. Great minds have provided us with many insights about true friendship, and their wisdom can enhance our own understanding of friendship and the role that it plays in attaining our highest mental and spiritual potential.

~~~~~

Perspectives from Great Minds
~~~~~

I care not for the man who would make the highest use of me short of an all–adventuring friendship.

Henry Thoreau, *Journals*

There are three kinds of friendships which are beneficial and three kinds which are harmful. Friendships with the upright, the truthful, and the well–informed are beneficial. Friendships with those that flatter, with those who compromise their principles, and those whose talk is clever are harmful. Have no friends who are not equal to yourself.

Confucius, *Analects*

There can be no friendship where there is no freedom. Friendship loves a free air, and will not be fenced up in straight and narrow enclosures.

William Penn, *Some Fruits of Solitude*

We are not to look for what makes friendships useful, but for whatever may be found in friendship that may lend utility to life.

George Santayana, *The Life of Reason*

The most I can do for my friend is simply to be his friend...If he knows that I am happy in loving him, he will want no other reward. Is not friendship divine in this?

Henry Thoreau, *Journals*

Friendship is the marriage of souls.

Voltaire, "Friendship"

The true friend is another self.

Cicero, *de Amicitia*

My true friends have come to me unsought. God gave them to me.

Ralph Waldo Emerson, "Friendship"

Insofar as friendship is a matter of the will, it cannot unite the two people.

Meister Eckhart, *Sermons*

Sometimes we are said to love another, that is, to stand in a true relation to our friend, so that we give the best to, and receive the best from, him. Between whom there is hearty truth, there is love, and in proportion to our truthfulness and confidence in one another, our lives are divine and miraculous, and answer to our ideal.

Henry Thoreau, *A Week on the
Concord and Merrimack Rivers*

A sound friendship permits the expression of a healthy amount of passivity, relaxation, and childishness...and since there is no danger and we are loved and respected for ourselves rather than for any front we put on or role we play, we can be as we really are.

Abraham Maslow, *Motivation and Personality*

Better be a thorn in the side of your friend than be his echo.

Ralph Waldo Emerson, "Friendship"

One has no friend who has many friends.

Aristotle, *Eudemian Ethics*

One friend in a lifetime is much; two are many; three are hardly possible.

Henry Adams, *The Education of Henry Adams*

We must accept or refuse one another as we are. I could tame a hyena more easily than my Friend. He is a material no tool of mine will work.

Henry Thoreau, *A Week on the Concord and Merrimack Rivers*

Friendship makes prosperity brighter, while it lightens adversity by sharing its griefs and anxieties.

Cicero, *de Amicitia*

Friendship demands a religious treatment. We talk of choosing our friends, but friends are self–elected. Reverence is a great part of it.

Ralph Waldo Emerson, "Friendship"

Friends will not only live in harmony, but in melody.

Henry Thoreau, *Journals*

UNCONDITIONAL LOVE

Love seeks no cause beyond itself and no fruit; is is its own fruit. I love you because I love you; I love in order that I may love.

St. Bernard

The deepest human need, according to Erich Fromm, is to overcome one's sense of separateness and to transcend one's own individual life and find *at–one–ment* with others. We usually speak of love as the process by which we leave our separateness and enter into true union with others. Our ego, however, often fears such a union, because it may lose its individual integrity in the process of uniting on an equal basis with others. Love, in this case, is conditioned by the ego's limitations, and we cannot fully overcome our separateness from others.

Unconditional love, on the other hand, is free of ego–driven conditions, and its essential message is one of complete liberation from self–centered preoccupations in the process of union with others. Unconditional love means we demonstrate to others that they can be whoever they are and express all their thoughts and feelings with the absolute confidence that our love for them will not be withdrawn. When love cannot be taken away, we are liberated to explore union without creating potential threats to the ego.

Unconditional love also allows both parties the freedom to maintain their individual integrity while uniting with each other. Here is the true paradox of unconditional love: two beings become one and yet remain two. When we experience unconditional love, we maintain our individual integrity while simultaneously overcoming our separateness and isolation from others. Great minds have explored this paradox for centuries, and their insights can illuminate our search for *at–one–ment.*

Perspectives from Great Minds

Accustomed long to contemplating love, I have forgotten all difference between myself and others.

Milarepa

Where love rules, there is no will to power.

Carl Jung, *Collected Works*

I believe that the reason of life is for each of us simply to grow in love.

Leo Tolstoy, *The Law of Love*

Only the complete man can love others.

Confucius, *Analects*

Love is the active concern for the life and the growth of that which we love.

Erich Fromm, *The Art of Loving*

Love seeketh not itself to please, nor for itself hath any care, but for another gives its ease, and builds a Heaven in Hell's despair.

William Blake, "The Clod and the Pebble"

Love and fear exclude each other.

Macrobius

The important thing is not to love me for your own sake— but to love me for myself.

St. Catherine of Siena

There is no remedy for love but to love more.

Henry Thoreau, *Journals*

Love is not primarily a relationship to a specific person; it is an *attitude*, an *orientation* of *character* which determines the relatedness of a person to the world as a whole, not toward one "object" of love.

Erich Fromm , *The Art of Loving*

The true meaning of love of one's neighbor is not that it is a command from God which we are to fulfill, but that through it and in it we meet God.

Martin Buber, *At the Turning*

If I truly love one person, I love all persons, I love the world, I love life.

Erich Fromm, *The Art of Loving*

Love is infallible; it has no errors, for all errors are the lack of love.

William Law, *The Spirit of Love*

Because of a lack of mutual love between people, all the calamities, usurpations, hatred, and animosity in the world have arisen.

Mo Tzu, *Universal Love*

Love must be as much a light as a flame.

Henry David Thoreau, *Letters*

Love is active penetration of the other person, in which my desire to know is stilled by union. In the act of fusion I know you, I know myself, I know everybody and I "know" nothing.

Erich Fromm, *The Art of Loving*

The last, the most blessed, the absolutely convincing evidence of love remains: love itself, which is known and recognized by the love in another. Like is known only by like. Only he who abides in love can recognize love, and in the same way his love is to be known.

Søren Kierkegaard, *Works of Love*

The best principle whereby a man can steer his course in this world, is that which will make his life at once honorable and happy: which is to love every man in the whole world as God does.

Thomas Traherne, *Christian Ethics*

In regard to all persons, have the same love, have the same indifference, whether relations or strangers. Detach your heart as much from the one as from the other.

St. John of the Cross

Love is the active concern for the life and the growth of that which we love.

Erich Fromm, *The Art of Loving*

Love for our Neighbor consists of three things: to desire the greater good of everyone; to do what good we can when we can; and to bear other's faults.

John Vianney

As we know, the Universe is One, and that is why there is Love.

Yang Shih

Love your neighbor as you love yourself.

Jesus, *Matthew 22:39*

MEDITATION & CONTEMPLATION

The soul becomes prudent by sitting and being quiet.

Aristotle, *Metaphysics*

The practice of meditation, like much ancient wisdom, often is misunderstood by the modern world. Some people perceive meditation to mean forsaking all earthly pleasures and retreating to a monastery or a remote Tibetan mountaintop where the whole day is spent in lotus position. Others may have been caught up in the many "easy paths to enlightenment" that are so prevalent in the marketplace today and believe these to be meditation.

Most great minds have realized that meditation is neither of these two extremes. Meditation, or contemplative prayer as some have called it, is an ancient process with numerous modern applications. Today, as in the past, people who develop meditative states of awareness enjoy greatly enhanced physical and spiritual well–being.

Meditation fosters physical health by reducing the toll that stress takes upon our body, a fact that has been demonstrated at the nation's leading medical schools. For example, Dr. Herbert Benson of Harvard Medical School has spent twenty years documenting meditation's effects upon his patients. He has observed increased physical wellness and resistance to disease among those who meditate.

Meditation also promotes development of the spiritual wisdom found within us by helping us find and listen to that "little small voice" frequently heard by great minds. Through the ages, many great minds have used a variety of formal and informal means to meditate so they could reach their full spiritual potential. They realize, however, that meditation requires great mental discipline and a commitment to the process, even if one does not obtain immediate results. If a person is patient and has sufficient motivation to meditate, he or she can develop the self–discipline necessary for meditation, just as great minds have done.

Perspectives from Great Minds

Meditation is one of the ways in which the spiritual man keeps himself awake.

Thomas Merton, *Thoughts in Solitude*

When the attention of the mind is completely carried off and turned away from the bodily senses, then there is this state called ecstasy…there the brightness of the Lord is seen.

St. Augustine, *The Literal Meaning of Genesis*

God–seeking people will go out in the way of contemplation, above reason, above distinction, and above their created being through an eternal intuitive gazing.

Jan van Ruusbroec, *Adornment of the Spiritual Marriage*

No means other than reflection can produce real spiritual knowing.

Aparokshanubhuti Upanishad

Where there is inner peace and meditation, there is neither anxiousness nor dissipation.

St. Francis of Assisi, *Admonitions*

It is sweet to let the mind unbend on occasion.

Horace, *Epodes*

How can you expect a harvest of thought from those who have not had a seed-time?

Henry David Thoreau, *Journals*

We are not forced to take wings to find God, but only have to seek solitude and to look within ourselves.

St. Teresa of Avila, *The Way of Perfection*

You pray best when the mirror of your soul is empty of every image except the image of God.

Thomas Merton, *Thoughts in Solitude*

No more agitations in the external world,
No more painting of the mind inwardly,
When your mind is like a perpendicular wall,
Then only can you enter into the realm of Reality.

Chinese Zen Master Bodhidharma

A life of only a single day spent in virtuous meditation is better than living a hundred years unbalanced.

Buddha, *Dhammapada*

Socrates: "The body is a source of endless trouble...to us in the search after truth."

Plato's *Phaedo*

Meditation is a powerful and full study for anyone who knows how to examine and exercise himself vigorously; I would rather fashion my mind than furnish it.

Montaigne, *Essays*

Just as rain leaks into a house with a poorly-made roof, desire and attachment will seep into a house unprotected by meditation.

Buddha, *Dhammapada*

Prayer achieves a sympathetic resonance with a more majestic force than man can control or comprehend.

Benjamin Franklin, *Rules for Self-Command*

Prayer oneth the soul with God.

St. Julian of Norwich, *Reflections of Divine Love*

Crito recalling Socrates: "Thought is best when the mind is gathered into itself and nothing troubles it — neither sounds nor sights, nor pain nor any pleasure — when it has as little as possible to do with the body...but is aspiring after being."

Plato's *Phaedo*

The days pass and are gone, and one finds that he never once had time to think...one who does not meditate cannot have wisdom.

Hasidic Leader Rabbi Nachman of Bratslav

Worship Me through meditation in the sanctuary of the heart.

Srimad Bhagavatam

The wise man remains wholly centered in himself.

Yogavasishtha

Meditation is a cleansing place for hearts from the strains of iniquities, and an opening to the door of the Mysteries.

Ibn 'Atâ'illâh, *Al-Hikam al-'Atâ'îyah*

When you pray, enter into your closet, and when you have shut the door, pray to God who is in secret.

Jesus, *Matthew 6:6*

The prayer of the monk is not perfect until he no longer realizes himself or that he is praying.

St. Anthony

Place your mind before the mirror of eternity!
Place your heart in the figure of the divine substance!
Transform your being into the image of God through
contemplation.

St. Clare of Assisi, *Third Letter to St. Agnes*

If we try to contemplate God without having turned the face
of our inner self entirely in God's direction, we will end up
inevitably by contemplating ourselves.

Thomas Merton, *Thoughts in Solitude*

The mind is a flighty and elusive, moving wherever it
pleases. Taming it is wonderful indeed — for a disciplined
mind invites true joy.

Buddha, *Dhammapada*

You should not be thinking of other things while speaking
with God, for doing so amounts to not knowing what
contemplation is.

St. Teresa of Avila, *The Way of Perfection*

Prayer... is the orientation of our whole body, mind, and
spirit to God in silence, attention, and adoration. All good
meditative prayer is a conversation of our entire self with
God.

Thomas Merton, *Thoughts in Solitude*

When the Gnostic's spiritual eye is opened, his bodily eye is
shut and he sees nothing but God.

Sufi Master Abû Sulaymân al-Dârânî

You must close the eyes and awaken in yourself that other
power of vision, the birthright of all, but which few turn to
use.

Plotinus, *Enneads*

One momentary glimpse of Divine Wisdom, born of meditation, is more precious than any amount of knowledge derived mainly from listening to and thinking about religious teachings.

Gampopa, *Rosary of Religious Gems*

The mind of the sage being in repose becomes the mirror of the universe.

Chuang Tzu

Truth rises from the silence of being quiet to the tremendous power of the Word.

Thomas Merton, *Thoughts in Solitude*

All the troubles of humanity come from our not knowing how to sit still.

Blaise Pascal, *Pensées*

As a flame standing in a windless place flickers not, so is the mind restrained in a place of infinite happiness. This happiness comes to one whose mind is fully tranquil and who has become one with God.

Bhagavadgita

External silence is most necessary to cultivate the internal; and indeed 'tis impossible to become inward without loving silence.

Madam Guyon, *A Method of Prayer*

Not only a truer knowledge, but a greater power comes to one in the quietude and silence of a mind that, instead of bubbling on the surface, can go to its own depths and listen.

Sri Aurobindo, *Letters*

ENLIGHTENED VISION

Nature seemed to me full of wonders, and I wanted to steep myself in them. Every stone, every plant, every single thing seemed alive and incredibly marvelous. I immersed myself in nature, crawled into the very essence of nature.

Carl Gustav Jung, *Memories, Dreams, Reflections*

"To see a world in a grain of sand" says William Blake in his poem, "Auguries of Innocence." Blake indicates in this and other passages his participation with countless other great minds in the secret of enlightened vision. Their perception of the universe transcends ordinary notions of reality that have created distinctions or boundaries between we humans and the rest of creation. Great minds break through these boundaries and experience the universal flow of life permeating every aspect of Nature. To these great minds, each and every atom of creation harmonizes and blends into a universal symphony which we all can learn to hear. As Ralph Waldo Emerson announced in his journals, "To the illuminated mind, the whole world sparkles with light."

Perspectives from Great Minds

Only in the state of enlightenment shall we be able to become one with all that lives. In this act of unification we liberate ourselves and all other living beings.

Lama Govinda, *Creative Meditations and Multi-Dimensional Consciousness*

The gate was opened to me that in one quarter of an hour I saw and knew more than if I had been many years at a university. For I saw and knew the being of all being... and all creatures through the divine wisdom.

Jacob Böhme

I saw that my spirit was borne to the heavens.... Then I became a bird whose body was of Oneness and whose wings were of Everlastingness, and I continued to fly in the air of the Absolute.

Sufi Mystic Abu Yazid

To see a World in a Grain of Sand,
And a Heaven in a Wild Flower,
Hold Infinity in the palm of your hand,
And Eternity in an hour.

William Blake, *"Auguries of Innocence"*

Think of our life in nature — daily to be shown matter, to come in contact with it, — rocks, trees, wind on our cheeks! the solid earth! the actual world! the common sense! Contact! Contact!

Henry David Thoreau, *Katahdin and the Maine Woods*

There are people on earth who live, not as dwellers thereon, but as observers of things heavenly and divine.

Cicero, *De Natura Deorum*

Isn't it almost an actual religion that the simple Japanese teach us, who live in nature as though they themselves were flowers?

Vincent van Gogh, *Letters*

In an instant, rise from time and space. Set the world aside and become a world within yourself.

Shabistari, *The Secret Garden*

"Sensible" people have no conception of the delight which the mere consciousness of living intensely can give: one's heart swells, one's imagination soars into space, life is inexpressively quickened, and one loses all consciousness of one's bodily limitations.

Hector Berlioz, *Autobiography*

The setting sun will always set me to rights — or if a sparrow comes before my window, I take part in its existence and pick about the gravel with it.

John Keats, *Letters*

In my breaking through...I transcend all creatures and am neither God nor creature...for in this breaking through I find that God and I are both the same.

Meister Eckhart, *Sermons*

I become a transparent eyeball; I am nothing. I see all; the currents of the Universal Being circulate through me; I am part or particle of God!

Ralph Waldo Emerson, *Nature*

God, I can push the grass apart and lay my finger on Thy heart!

Edna St. Vincent Millay, *" Renascence"*

The universe is a more amazing puzzle than ever, as you glance along this bewildering series of animated forms...I feel the centipede in me — cayman, carp, eagle, and fox. I am moved by strange sympathies.

Ralph Waldo Emerson, *Journals*

I live not in myself, but I become portion of that around me; and to me High mountains are a feeling...Are not the mountains, waves, and skies a part of me and my soul, as I them?

George Gordon, Lord Byron, *Childe Harold's Pilgrimage*

The moon is the same old moon,
The flowers exactly as they were,
Yet I've become the thingness
Of all the things that I see!

Zen Master Bunan

When "childlikeness" is attained, man thinks yet he does not think. He thinks like the showers coming down from the sky; he thinks like the waves rolling on the ocean, he thinks like the stars illuminating the nightly heavens.... Indeed he is the showers, the ocean, the stars.

Shunryu Suzuki, *"Introduction" to Zen and the Art of Archery*

At times I feel as if I am spread out over the landscape and inside things, and am myself living in every tree, in the splashing of waves, in the clouds and animals that come and go, in the procession of the seasons.

Carl Gustav Jung, *Memories, Dreams, Reflections*

I was suddenly sensible of such sweet and beneficent society in Nature, in the very patterning of the raindrops, and in every sound and sight around my house, an infinite and unaccountable friendliness all at once like an atmosphere sustaining me.

Henry David Thoreau, *Walden*

Now I was come up in spirit, through the flaming sword to the Paradise of God. All things were new... beyond what words can utter.

George Fox, *Journals*

Free thinker! Do you think you are the only thinker on this earth in which life blazes?... Look carefully in an animal at a spirit alive; every flower is a soul opening out into nature.

Gérard de Nerval, *"Golden Lines"*

What I know of the divine sciences and Holy Scriptures, I learned in woods and fields. I have no other masters than the beeches and oaks...Trees and stones will teach you more than you can acquire from the mouth of a magister.

                    St. Bernard

There was a time when meadow, grove, and stream,
The earth, and every common sight, to me did seem
Apparelled in celestial light,
The glory and freshness of a dream.

    William Wordsworth, *"Ode: Intimations of Immortality"*

Lo, the poor Indian; whose untutored mind
Sees God in clouds, or hears God in the wind.

          Alexander Pope, *Essay on Man*

All objects within my gaze trembled and vibrated...My body, Master's, the courtyard, the furniture and floor, the trees and sunshine...all melted into a luminescent sea, an oceanic joy broke upon calm endless shores of my soul.

      Paramhansa Yogananda, *Autobiography of a Yogi*

I was born with a divine jewel,
Long since filmed over with dust.
This morning, wiped clean, it mirrors
Streams and mountains without end.

        Chinese Zen Master Ikuzanchu

I was sitting by the ocean...when I suddenly became aware of my whole environment as being engaged in a gigantic cosmic dance...I "saw" cascades of energy coming down from outer space in which particles were created and destroyed in rhythmic pulses.

          Fritjof Capra, *The Tao of Physics*

The Dust and Stones of the Street were as Precious as GOLD...their sweetness and unusual Beauty made my heart to leap...Eternity was manifest in the Light of the Day.

Thomas Traherne, *Centuries of Meditation*

The great lesson from the true mystics, from the Zen monks, and now also from the Humanistic and Transpersonal psychologists is that the sacred is in the ordinary, that it is to be found in one's daily life...in one's own backyard.

Abraham Maslow, *The Further Reaches of Human Nature*

The wind blows hard among the pines toward the beginning of an endless past. Listen: You've heard everything.

Shinkichi Takahashi, *"Wind Among the Pines"*

From my own unforgettable experience I know very well that there is a state in which the bonds of the personal nature of life seem to have fallen away from us and we experience an undivided unity.

Martin Buber, *Between Man and Man*

Overcoming of all the usual barriers between the individual and the Absolute is the greatest mystical achievement. In mystic experiences, we both become one with the Absolute and we become aware of our oneness.

William James, *The Varieties of Religious Experience*

If you pass beyond form, O friends, 'tis Paradise and rose gardens within rose gardens. When you have broken and destroyed your own form, you have learned to break the form of everything.

Rumi, *Masnavi*

We cannot comprehend spiritual things with ordinary intelligence.

The Gospel of Sri Ramakrishna

GAIA, OUR EARTH MOTHER

For ancient people, nature was not just a treasure-trove of natural resources. Nature was a goddess, Mother Earth; the whole environment was divine.

Arnold Toynbee

One of the most profound events during the year 1988 was an international gathering of biological, physical, and geological scientists in San Diego. These scientists studied new evidence that Earth's biosphere actually may be more than just the aggregate of all living things; it may include the Earth itself as a distinct living entity. *The Earth is alive?* Yes, the planet itself may possess certain life characteristics similar to those taught to biology students everywhere. While this perspective may be new and provocative to the scientific community, it certainly is not to many of the world's most ancient civilizations who did not question the Earth's being alive.

The Greeks, for example, used the term *GAIA* to describe our Earth Mother as a spiritual entity possessing a distinct life of her own. Africans knew the Earth as an intimate friend with its own personality, a friend with whom they were in constant communication. Native Americans have had similar respect for the planet as a distinct life force, as have many of the world's greatest minds.

To these people, the Earth is not a mere "thing" to be plundered callously; the Earth is the mother/friend/nurturer who not only provides our physical needs, but also teaches us profound spiritual lessons. Ancient wisdom may soon unite with our modern scientific wisdom in the awareness that our planet is, indeed, "alive" and must be treated with reverence.

Perspectives from Great Minds

Let us admit that this world is a living being who has a soul; that it is a spiritual being and that, in truth, it has been engendered by the Providence of God.

Plato, *Timaeus*

The Earth, its life am I
The Earth, its body is my body
The Earth, its thoughts are my thoughts.

Navajo Song

The earth that supports all, whose heart is in the highest heaven; immortal, surrounded by truth, shall bestow upon us brilliancy and strength... Oh, Mother Earth!

Athara Veda

We see on Mother Earth the running streams,
We see the promise of her fruitfulness.
Truly, her power she gives us.
Our thanks to Mother Earth!

The Hako Ceremony Song of the Pawnee People

I will sing of well-founded Earth, mother of all, eldest of all beings. She feeds all creatures that are in the world...Hail mother of the Gods!

The Homeric Hymns

We thank our mother, the Earth, whom we claim as mother because the Earth causes us and everything we need.

"New Year, Big House" Ceremonial Prayer
of the Lenape (Delaware) People

Injury to the earth is like striking, cutting, maiming, or killing a blind man.... He who understands the nature of sin against the earth is called a true sage.

Acaranga Sutra

Those honor Nature well, who teach that she can speak on everything, even on theology.

Blaise Pascal, *Pensées*

Forget not that the earth delights to feel your bare feet and the winds long to play with your hair.

Kahil Gibran, *The Prophet*

Earth, with her thousand voices, praises God.

Samuel Taylor Coleridge, "Hymn Before Sunrise"

To him who in the love of Nature holds
Communion with her visible forms, she speaks
A various language.

William Cullen Bryant, "Thanatopsis"

Nature, with equal mind,
Sees all her sons at play;
Sees man control the wind,
The wind sweeps man away.

Matthew Arnold, "Empedocles on Etna"

Oh Mother Earth, you are the earthly source of all existence. The fruits you bear are the source of life for all the Earth peoples... May the steps we take in life upon you be sacred and not weak.

Prayer of the Oglala Sioux

The mother of all our songs bore us in the beginning of all things. To our mother alone do we belong.

Song of the Kagaba People of Colombia

The natural world is like a spiritual house...
Man walks there through forests of physical things
        that are also spiritual things,
That watch him with affectionate looks.

Charles Baudelaire, "Intimate Associations"

He prays to the spirit of the place and to the Earth, the first of the gods.

Virgil, *Aeneid*

The earth is not a mere fragment of dead history...but a living earth; compared with whose great central life all animal and vegetative life is merely parasitic.

Henry David Thoreau, *Walden*

The Golden Rule applies not only to the dealings of human individuals and human societies with one another, but also to their dealings with other living creatures and with the planet upon which we are all traveling through space and time.

Aldous Huxley, *Literature and Science*

I am a son of the Earth, the soil is my mother...may she lavish on me her manifested treasure, her secret riches.

Atharva Veda

Shall I not have intelligence with the earth? Am I not partly leaves and vegetable mould myself?

Henry David Thoreau, *Walden*

Naked you came from the Earth, our Mother. Naked you return to her. May a good wind be your road.

Omaha Prayer for the Deceased

CO-CREATION

And out of the ground God formed every beast of the field and every bird of the sky, and brought them to the man to see what he would call them; and whatever the man called a living creature, that was its name.

Genesis, Chapter 2 verses 19

Western religions might look to this verse from *Genesis* and observe God as the only source of creation. Unfortunately, by focusing exclusively upon the divine aspect of the creative process, they would miss the important role that Adam, as a symbol for all humanity, plays in creation. Adam *names* the animals, a conscious process which utilizes our greatest asset, the mind. Carl Jung recognized humanity's role in the creative process and maintained that human destiny ultimately lies in the creation of more and more consciousness out of the depths of the unconscious mind, a parallel in many ways to God's creating matter out of the ineffable void. In other words, to fulfill our destiny, we must join God, the Universal Creative Essence, as co–creators of reality by increasing consciousness and using it to participate in the evolutionary patterning of our planet.

Perhaps you may be wondering what possible value could lie in creating consciousness. Teilhard de Chardin provides an answer: "In human beings, the evolution of the world towards the Spirit becomes conscious. From that moment on, our perfection, our interest, our salvation as elements of creation only can be to press on with this evolution with all our strength." Consciousness is humanity's flower; it is our unique way of expressing the loving spiritual presence within us. It also is the God–given tool we must wield in the creative process. Great minds have recognized their roles as co–creators, and their wisdom can help us fulfill our destiny.

Perspectives from Great Minds

Creation does not merely take place only in the beginning, but also at every moment throughout the whole of time...All of us created in the image of God are potentially able to become images of the Divine.

Martin Buber, *The Way of Response*

The universe came into being with us together; with us, all things are one.

Chuang Tzu, *Basic Writings*

If there is a good and wise God, then there also exists a progress of humanity towards perfection.

Plato

The history of humanity seems to demonstrate the emergence of our progressively conscious participation in universal evolution.

Buckminster Fuller, *No More Secondhand God*

People have never fully used the powers they possess to advance the good in life because they have waited upon some power external to themselves to do the work they are responsible for doing.

John Dewey

In a manner which exceeds description and thought, the man of God is found worthy to become not God, but what God is; that is to say, man becomes what God is by nature.

William of St. Thierry, *The Golden Epistle*

I believe I shall some time cease to be an individual, and that the eternal tendency of the soul is to become universal.

Ralph Waldo Emerson, *Journals*

The simple truth is that there has lived on Earth—appearing at different intervals—for thousands of years among ordinary people, the faint beginnings of another race; walking the Earth and breathing the air with us...This new race is in the act of being born from us, and in the near future, will occupy and possess the Earth.

Edmund Bucke, *Cosmic Consciousness*

Each animal and vegetable form remembers the next inferior one and predicts the next higher one.

Ralph Waldo Emerson, *"Poetry and Imagination "*

Evolution of consciousness is the central motive of terrestrial existence.

Sri Aurobindo, *The Future Evolution of Man*

Once we push the gate of the mind slightly ajar and let the light stream in, the meaning of life becomes silently revealed to us... We draw back, surprised... man as a spiritual being possesses a capacity for wisdom which is infinite.

Paul Brunton, *The Secret Path*

Entering space will demand comprehension of the universe's laws. Man will become a conscious participant in his own evolution.

Buckminster Fuller, I *Seem to Be a Verb*

With freedom of choice and with honor, as though the maker and molder of thyself... thou shalt have the power out of thy soul's judgement, to be born into the higher forms.

Pico della Mirandola

When you have become one with the Great Universal, you will have no partiality, and when you are part of the process of transformation, you will have no rigidity.

Confucius

Man's capacities have never been measured; nor are we to judge what we can do by any precedents, so little has been tried.

Henry David Thoreau, *Walden*

Everywhere on Earth, at this moment, there floats in a sea of mutual sensitivity, love of God and faith in the world; the two essential ingredients of the Ultrahuman.

Teilhard de Chardin, *The Phenomenon of Man*

The new humanity will be universal and it will have the artist's attitude: that is, it will recognize that the immense value and beauty of the human being lie precisely in that he belongs to the two kingdoms, nature and spirit.

Thomas Mann, in *What I Believe*

The human individual usually lives far within his limits; he possesses powers of various sorts which he habitually fails to use. He energizes below his maximum.

William James, Essay: *"The Energies of Man"*

Progress is the law of human life; the human is not human as yet.

Robert Browning, *"Paracelsus"*

Humans first appeared as fishes. When they were able to help themselves, they took to dry land.

Anaximander

I know of no more encouraging fact than the unquestionable ability of man to elevate his life by conscious endeavor.

Henry David Thoreau, *Walden*

A new world where men and things will know harmonious relationships.

Francis Ponge, *Appendix to the Notebook of the Pine Woods*

Man is a creature who has received the order to become God.

St. Basil, Bishop of Caesarea

If you possess true knowledge (*gnosis*), O Soul, you will understand that you are akin to your creator.

Hermes, *Libellus*

Man is a rope stretched between the animal and the Superhuman.

Nietzsche, T*hus Spoke Zarathustra*

If then, being made of Life and Light, you learn to know that you are made from them, you will go back into Life and Light.

Hermes, *Libellus*

One who is renewed by daily progressing in the knowledge of God is converting the direction of his love from the temporal to the eternal, from carnal to spiritual things.

St. Augustine, *On the Truth*

If the people of the future are better than we are, they will, perhaps, look back at us with feelings of pity and tenderness for struggling souls who once divined a little of what the future would bring.

George Sand, *Intimate Journal 1834*

Only man, with his conscious intellect, has been able to continue his evolution after his biological development has finished... he approaches the state where what he wills may be done.

W. H. Auden, in *What I Believe*

Our secret creative will divines its counterpart in others, experiencing its own universality.

Dag Hammarskjöld, *Markings*

The sense of our real powers which we seem to derive from the universe itself comes and goes... We are reluctant to talk about this because there is nothing we can prove.

Saul Bellow, *Nobel Prize Acceptance Speech*

The mind of man is capable of anything because everything is in it, all the past as well as the future.

Joseph Conrad, *Heart of Darkness*

When grace draws us to contemplation, it seems to transfigure us even physically...we now appear changed and lovely to behold...so that good people are honored and delighted to be in our company, strengthened by the sense of God we radiate.

The Cloud of Unknowing

God sleeps in minerals, awakens in plants, and thinks in humans.

from an ancient Sanskrit text

WHAT THEN MUST WE DO?

I don't know what your destiny will be, but one thing I know: the only ones among you who will be truly happy are those who will have sought and found how to serve.

Albert Schweitzer, *The Philosophy of Civilization*

Confronted with the devastating poverty in his beloved Moscow, Leo Tolstoy compassionately distributed his considerable wealth to people in the streets. In spite of his well-intentioned generosity, the poverty remained unabated prompting Tolstoy to proclaim, "What then must we do?" Tolstoy's dilemma has confronted the sensitivities of great minds for thousands of years. Today it confronts each of us as we witness pervasive injustice and suffering in our own midst as well as in remote corners of the world.

As we progress along our life's path, we may discover inner stirring of compassion for any part of creation that is suffering; however, we want to know that our compassion will lead us to appropriate service in accordance with our talents and resources. We must ask the truth dwelling within us to help unite the unbridled idealism of Don Quixote's "Impossible Dream" with the effort and selfless commitment of Albert Schweitzer, Gandhi, and Mother Teresa. Then— and only then—will we know the answer to Tolstoy's question.

Perspectives from Great Minds

It is better to light one small candle than to curse the darkness.

Confucius, *Analects*

The aim of life is self-development.To realize one's nature perfectly—that is what each of us is here for.

Oscar Wilde, *The Portrait of Dorian Gray*

To achieve unity among people, we must cultivate it within ourselves; to enact that unity, we must have a vision of it before our eyes.

Lewis Mumford, *The Transformations of Man*

The lightening spark of thought generated in the solitary mind awakens its likeness in another mind.

Thomas Carlyle, *Essays*

We were born to unite with other people and to join in comity with the human race.

Cicero, *De finibus*

Divine knowledge is not to be borrowed from books. It has to be realized in oneself. Books are at best an aid, often a hindrance.

Gandhi

Knowledge, if it does not determine action, is dead to us.

Plotinus, *Enneads*

It is impossible to solve problems belonging to a higher level of consciousness from the point of view of a lower level of consciousness.

Lama Govinda, *Creative Meditation and
Multi-dimensional Consciousness*

A little knowledge which you carry out in action is more profitable than much knowledge which you neglect to carry out in action.

Hermes, *De Castogatione Animae*

It is not after we understand the truth that we attain enlightenment. To realize the truth is to live — to exist here and now.

Shunryu Suzuki, *Zen Mind, Beginners Mind*

All methods and techniques — and of course all human beings who propound them — are merely instruments to help the student attain a methodless, technique-free, teacherless state.

Paul Brunton, *The Wisdom of the Overself*

At that point in your life where your talent meets the needs of the world, that is where God wants you to be.

Albert Schweitzer, *The Philosophy of Civilization*

All that a man has to say or do that can possibly concern mankind, is in some shape or other, to tell the story of his love — to sing; and if he is fortunate and keeps alive, he will forever be in love. This alone is to be alive.

Henry Thoreau, *Journals*

We have it in our power to begin the world again.

Thomas Paine, *Common Sense*

If you want to have a spiritual life you must unify your life. A life is either all spiritual or not spiritual at all.

Thomas Merton, *Thoughts in Solitude*

Success as the ultimate concern is not the natural desire of actualizing potentialities.

Paul Tillich, *Dynamics of Faith*

The true value of a human being is determined by the measure and sense in which one has attained liberation from the self.

Albert Einstein, *My World Picture*

It is too easy to find an excuse for inaction by pleading the decadence of civilization, or the imminent end of the world. This defeatism, whether it be innate or a mere affection,... seems to be the besetting temptation of our time.

Teilhard de Chardin, *Building the Earth*

There must come about a spiritualizing of the masses. The mass of individuals must know how to reflect about their lives and what they want to secure for their lives.

Albert Schweitzer, *The Philosophy of Civilization*

There are moments in your life when you must act, even though you cannot carry your best friends with you. The "still small voice" within you must always be the final arbiter where there is a conflict of duty.

Gandhi

You give but little when you give of your possessions. It is when you give of yourself that you truly give.

Kahil Gibran

If I can stop one heart form breaking, I shall not live in vain.

Emily Dickinson, *"Life"*

When I am no longer involved in the measurement of life, but in the living of it ...my whole life becomes a prayer.

Thomas Merton, *Thoughts in Solitude*

Let knowledge grow from more to more
But more of reverence in us dwell;
That mind and soul, according well,
May make one music as before.

Alfred, Lord Tennyson, *"In Memoriam A. H. H."*

An individual has not started living until he can rise above the narrow confines of individualistic concerns to the broader concerns of all humanity.

Martin Luther King, Jr., *Words of M. L. King, Jr.*

Because the superior person is serious about what is in himself, he progresses every day. Because the inferior person neglects what is in himself, he retrogresses every day.

Hsun Tzu

I believe him liberated forever who performs every act without the idea of his personally doing it, taking it to be only a part of the multifarious spontaneous action of Nature.

Yogavasishtha

You must be one person, good or bad; you must develop either your Governing Principle or your outward attributes; you must study either your inner being or outward things.

Epictetus, *The Encheiridion*

Aspiration alone is not enough. It must be backed by discipline, training, and endeavor...Every act is to be brought into the field of awareness and done deliberately.

Paul Brunton, *Notebook One*

No spiritual mind remains within itself; it is always aspiring and going beyond its own strength.

Montaigne, *Essays*

Only those who develop their minds and spirits to the utmost can serve Heaven and fulfill their own destinies.

Mencius

The more you advance toward God, the less God will give you worldly duties to perform.

Sri Ramakrishna

PART THREE:
MORE TECHNIQUES FROM GREAT MINDS

- **Exercises to Nurture a Childlike Nature**

  The Renaissance Rorschach — da Vinci

  Kleevision — Paul Klee

  Collage Creation — Miró *et al*

  A Child's Eye–View — Turner *et al*

- **Exercises to Promote Self–knowledge, Self–awareness, and Self–acceptance**

  Symbols for Feelings — Carl Jung

  A Constellation of You

  Writing a Personal Myth

  Portrait of a Good Decision

- **Exercises to Promote Present Tense Awareness**

  Describe Out Loud — Goethe and Whistler

  Here and Now of Awareness

  Beach Sand Writing

  Creating and Using Affirmations

- **Exercises to Enhance Meditation and Contemplation**

  Four Step Meditation Program

  Camera Obscura — Percy Shelley

  Illumination

  Energy Bubble Visualization

  Inner Guide Visualization — Carl Jung

- **Exercises to Help Us Answer the Question: "What Then Must We Do?"**

  Determining Priorities — Henry Thoreau

  Walking the Spiritual Path

EXERCISES: RECOVERING OUR IMAGINATIVE, CHILDLIKE NATURE

Buckminster Fuller once commented that all children are born a genius—they just get "de-geniused" very quickly. Abraham Maslow confirms Fuller's sagacity and maintains that unlimited creative potential is a birthright of our species, not something reserved for those whom we typically have hailed as being gifted. Maslow calls our innate creativity "primary creativeness" because we possess it at birth. Primary creativeness entails characteristics most children possess: an active imagination, natural inquisitiveness, playfulness, and spontaneity. Maslow believes that primary creativeness produces creative inspiration and that adults who have maintained their primary creativeness tend to be the most creative members of society. Likewise, those who have distanced themselves from their innate primary creativeness become, as Fuller quipped, "de–geniused."

Recent tests measuring creativity in children and adults confirm Fuller's observation. Tests indicate that the average child's creativity begins to diminish significantly around the age six or seven. Jean Piaget's work with mental skills development in children indicates that this is the age at which children generally develop rational and logical thought processes. Maslow calls logic and rationality "secondary processes," since they are not present at birth. Children acquire secondary thought processes from parents, teachers, and other adults who already are using these processes. Because we use logical and rational processes to criticize, evaluate, and judge our ideas and experiences, these mental activities often inhibit or restrict our innate playful and inquisitive nature.

Once secondary processes emerge, society provides positive reinforcement for their development which further erodes our primary creativeness. For example, our educational system uses grades to reward children who are most adept at learning the logical and rational skills needed in reading, mathematics, science, and other classes. Unfortunately, few positive reinforcements, and often many negative ones, are given for playful, imaginative, or divergent thinking. Even art classes can stifle primary creativeness as teachers encourage children to abandon their imaginative, natural drawing style and to "color inside the lines." Through time many people lose contact with their primary creativeness and with the playful, childlike nature that once was so natural. Our birthright, our childlike creativeness, shrivels up inside us as we struggle to cope with an adult world governed by logic and reason.

Modern research indicates, however, that even if we have lost contact with the childlike creativeness within us we can awaken it and regain our birthright. Rollo May, like Maslow, maintains that creative people have somehow been able to maintain or re-establish contact with their childlike primary creativeness in spite of societal reinforcement given to logical and rational skills. These eminent psychologists feel that adults who have remained open to their childlike nature or who have rekindled it are society's most well-adjusted and fully integrated human beings. These people have united a child's imaginative spontaneity with an adult's logical faculties. Their unbridled imagination furnishes them with creative inspiration that the evaluative, goal–directed logical processes can develop and bring into reality. These are our great minds, our examples of fully developed creative potential.

If we desire to develop our own creative potential as the great minds have done, then we must nurture our childlike nature. We also must overcome our dependency upon the secondary processes and their tendency to judge, evaluate, and criticize our life experiences. Fortunately, many great minds recorded in their journals and notebooks the actual techniques they used to rekindle any portion of their childlike nature they had lost. Several of these techniques will follow this discussion. We also are fortunate that creativity researchers have identified the particular environment in which creative potential is most likely to blossom.

Conditions that Nurture Our Innate Creativity

- **Self–acceptance**
- **Heightened awareness**
- **Tolerance of Ambiguous or Unfamiliar Experiences**
- **An Internal Locus of Evaluation**
- **The Ability to "Play" with Experience**

Self–acceptance

"I exist as I am, that is enough. If no other in the world be aware, I sit content. And if each and all be aware, I sit content."

Walt Whitman's *Song of Myself* celebrates self–acceptance. Each person offers great potential to humanity, and acceptance of ourselves as unique expressions of human potential frees us to offer our ideas to each other without concern about being judged or rejected. Most young children remain free from other people's opinions and judgments. They are naturally spontaneous and expressive, even at the risk of appearing foolish. Their primary concern is to explore the world around them in whatever fashion they deem appropriate at the moment.

As adults desiring to activate our potential, we, too, should not be overly concerned with other people's opinions. (Refer to the Secret concerning Self–acceptance and the Self–acceptance Exercises in Part 3.) Even if we occasionally think or act inappropriately, we can learn from these experiences and move forward. Life is a journey, not a popularity contest. Acceptance of who you are at any point in your journey is fundamental to developing your innate creative potential.

Heightened Awareness

Buckminster Fuller attributed much of his success to his constant self–questioning about what was the most important thing happening around him during "each and every extraordinary moment of the day." He, other great minds, and most children recognize the importance of "now-centered" awareness which enables us to have meaningful encounters with objects and life experiences. Each moment of our lives offers potential learning opportunities to us. Not one moment need be wasted or cast aside, if we learn to acquire Fuller's perspective. Participating in the "now" is fundamental to enhancing our creative potential. (Refer to Secret on Nowness and Being and the Present Tense Awareness Exercises in Part 3.)

Openness to Ambiguous or Unfamiliar Experiences

Openness to ambiguous or unfamiliar experiences reduces the mind's tendency to reject ideas or concepts outside its current understanding. It allows us to draw information from our experiences without forming mental judgments that would preclude broadening our understanding. Ellen Langer's book, *Mindfulness*, calls the tendency to make judgments before we have had adequate time to experience a new or unfamiliar encounter "premature cognitive commitment." In other words, when we face a new or unfamiliar encounter, we render a judgment of like or dislike, usefulness or uselessness, based more upon our pre–existing mindset than upon the new encounter's potential merits. We are guilty of making a decision based upon insufficient evidence, and our penalty is diminished creative potential and what Langer describes as "mindlessness."

Creative people, on the other hand, demonstrate "mindfulness," because they remain open to new experiences. Creative people have learned that few experiences lack an opportunity to expand thinking in some way.

Remaining open to new and unusual experiences helps produce an environment in which creative potential thrives.

An Internal Locus of Evaluation

Carl Rogers feels that someone who produces a new idea or creation must establish its value to him or herself without concern for other people's opinions of it. He believes that tempering our own ideas with other people's judgments erects barriers between ourselves and our creations. These barriers limit our ability to learn from our creative expressions. This does not mean we must be insensitive to other people's opinions. It simply means that we establish our own value for our ideas and creations, even if others hold different opinions. We must be free to "color outside the lines," even if others do not understand, if that is what our childlike nature tells us is appropriate for the moment.

The Ability to "Play" with Experience

As French poet Charles Baudelaire stated, "genius is nothing more than childhood recovered at will." Baudelaire and other great minds recognize that adults can recover their innate childlike creative nature, since it is a matter of *will*. They also recognize the tremendous impact that a playful, imaginative attitude has upon creativity. Creative people tend to play spontaneously with ideas, colors, shapes, relationships, and patterns they encounter. They are inherently curious about almost everything around them, and they let their innate curiosity guide their explorations of the world. The willingness to let go and "play," no matter how foolish or unusual something might seem, is fundamental to creativity. Great minds have not been threatened with looking foolish to others, and they actively sought to recover their childhood at will.

SUMMARY: Nurturing our Innate Creativity

These five elements (self–acceptance, heightened awareness, tolerance of ambiguity, internal locus of evaluation, and the ability to play) produce a fertile environment to rekindle our innate primary creativeness. Even if we feel that we have lost contact with our innate creativity, we can re-establish communication links with it just as many great minds have done. The exercises that follow were the methods they used to recover their own childhood at will.

— EXERCISES —

The Renaissance Rorschach — Leonardo da Vinci

GOAL: To stimulate mental flexibility and imaginative thinking.

The exemplary Renaissance Person, for many people, is Leonardo da Vinci. Few minds have contributed more to humanity than has this great artist, scientist, and philosopher. For centuries, Leonardo has been the subject of many inquiries seeking to uncover the methods and techniques responsible for his extensive creative activities. Although a shroud of mystery still cloaks his inner workings, his journals reveal a technique that was, perhaps, his most important and often used. Leonardo employed the technique both to stimulate his imagination and to stretch his mind and keep it in shape.

Two prominent investigators of Leonardo's accomplishments, Sigmund Freud and Paul Valéry, attribute his success to his active imagination. Valéry's conclusion was that Leonardo's imagination gave him remarkable perspective upon common, everyday experiences. He used these new perspectives to generate the discoveries and ideas for which he is famous. Leonardo's notebooks reveal the actual technique he used to stimulate his imagination. He describes his technique:

I cannot forbear to mention a new device for study which, although it may seem trivial and almost ludicrous, is extremely useful in arousing the mind to various inventions. And this is, when you look at a wall spotted with stains, or a mixture of stones, you may discover a resemblance to various landscapes; or again you may see battles and figures in action; in all, an endless variety of objects.

— The Key —

Leonardo, when using this technique, would let his sensory perceptions stimulate his imagination. He then could "see" various images, shapes, and objects emerge from the randomness of the cracks and stains. Later, if he desired, he could evaluate the images and associations he made and glean any insights produced through unbridled imaginative thinking. Or, at the very least, the technique afforded him an opportunity to stimulate and stretch his mind.

Fortunately, we can adapt Leonardo's technique to our contemporary needs. You might be thinking, "When will I ever find the time to sit and look at a pile of rocks or the cracks in the sidewalk to stretch my imagination?" Relax! You have sufficient time *right now*; it just is not being used for this purpose. Each of us encounters "blank time" during the routine hustle of modern living. For example, waiting in line creates blank time.

Waiting in line at the bank, cleaners, grocery store, on the freeway, or any of the other "holding patterns" we face, provides us with ample opportunities to use Leonardo's technique—*without taking one moment from our schedules.* Think what a blessing it would be if we used this blank time more productively. Instead of becoming tense or frustrated —known assassins of creativity—we could use that "lost" time as a launching pad for our creativity. We also can use the technique at other times to stimulate imaginative thinking and mental flexibility. The following are suggested means to utilize Leonardo's technique in your own creative needs:

Variation 1

Place a pencil, pen, or crayon in your hand in a manner in which you do not normally hold it. For example, try placing it between your little finger and the one next to it. Randomly—*without any thought as to what it will or should look like*—draw 12 to 15 lines on a piece of blank paper. Let the lines form themselves without providing any conscious direction. After you finish drawing lines, allow your imagi nation to generate images from the interrelationship of the lines, just as Leonardo did with cracks and stains. See any possible images that you feel the lines suggest. Don't judge or criticize; *whatever* you see is fine. You, like Leonardo, may see landscapes, battle scenes, faces, or other "concrete" objects. You also may experience subjective impressions or feelings such as feeling delighted, anxious, cheerful, energetic, sorrowful, etc. Our imagination can furnish both concrete images and subjective impressions.

Be aware that the goal is to stimulate the imagination—not create works of art. You may view the paper from various angles, crumple or fold it, or treat in any other manner you feel is appropriate. To extend this activity, try writing, drawing, or using other means to gain insight from your imaginative associations. Record in your journal any thoughts or impressions that you have generated while using Leonardo's technique.

Variation 2

Try the above activity with another person. View both your own and your friend's paper. Compare your findings. What do you notice? Verbalize your ideas and associations to each other. Remember to avoid criticism or an "I don't know how you see that!" attitude. Whatever you "see" will strengthen the imagination. Record your thoughts and impressions.

Variation 3

Be on the constant lookout for interesting buildings, geological formations, clouds, spider's webs, floor tiles, cracks in the sidewalk or ceiling, etc. with which you can use this technique. As children, we found the world filled with wonder and could spend hours engaged in imaginative thinking. Great minds such as Leonardo continued imaginative play throughout their lives, because they realized the importance of keeping the imagination alive. Also, remember to use this technique while waiting in line or during other "blank times!" In closing, we should heed Leonardo's advice:

> Iron rusts from disuse,
> stagnant water loses its purity;
> even so does inactivity
> sap the vigor from our minds.

TURN ON YOUR "KLEEVISION"
— PAUL KLEE

Igor Stravinsky once commented that truly creative people always strive to "insult habit." Arthur Koestler concurs with Stravinsky and feels that every creative act requires "a new innocence of perception, liberated from the cataract of accepted belief." These two great minds realize that if we shackle our perception with conventional or routine modes of awareness, our creative expression will be quite limited, if not altogether impossible. Tradition and habit can create "mindlessness" which diminishes our creative potential.

Koestler's metaphorical reference to the cataract of accepted belief pinpoints a major problem we face regarding creativity. A cataract builds up over time and its effects slowly become obvious, because the accumulation goes almost unnoticed until the cataract reduces our vision significantly. Likewise, the layers of accepted beliefs, habit, and routine which our culture heaps upon us as we mature gradually accumulate until they have reduced our awareness, often to the point of mindlessness. Our childlike, playful primary creativeness eventually yields to routine and habit, so we can cope with the demands of the accepted reality. Fortunately, we can remove both cataracts and habitual ways of perceiving and thinking.

Artist Paul Klee discovered a means to remove his own "cataracts of habitual perception" that could have limited his creative expression. The technique he developed to liberate his awareness involved temporarily altering his vision. Klee often used binoculars or other types of lenses to explore potential subjects for his work. The binoculars created an altered, somewhat distorted perspective of the subject. Klee felt this altered perspective freed his mind to uncover subtle nuances about the subject that an ordinary perspective may have overlooked. These new perspectives were a fertile territory for his imagination to explore. Occasionally Klee used the technique to give his mind a playful stretch, just as Leonardo stretched his mind with his technique.

We can employ variations of Klee's technique to give us new perspectives on familiar objects or simply to stretch our minds. There are three primary objectives for this exercise and you may use the variations of Klee's technique to address any of them. Use the suggested follow–up activities to stimulate additional insights.

OBJECTIVES FOR USING KLEEVISION

OBJECTIVE 1. To obtain fresh new perspectives for objects with which you are already familiar.

OBJECTIVE 2. To explore objects with which you are not familiar using new means of awareness.

OBJECTIVE 3. To engage in playful, open-ended perception to keep the mind active and stimulated.

PROCEDURE FOR KLEEVISION

1. Use a variety of "readymade" lenses to create new perspectives.

Try using binoculars, telescopes, camera lenses, magnifying glasses, etc. Look through both ends of the lenses. Hold the lenses at various angles. Use a variety of lenses on the camera (wide angle, telephoto, macro-focusing). Describe your observations aloud while using the readymade lenses. Draw or write down your ideas and insights. Use the follow-up activities for additional insight.

2. Create lenses.

Use drinking glasses, soft drink bottles, antique glass, glass bricks, etc. Use images reflected by objects such as stainless steel mixing bowls, aluminum foil, fun house mirrors, or any other reflective surface. A little distortion actually helps liberate perception!

3. Alter other senses to liberate them as well.

For hearing: try listening through a teacup, a towel, a marshmallow, a piece of newspaper, etc.

For touch: try wearing different socks on your hand, use your elbow to feel silk, use your toes to feel a bowl of Cheerios, etc. Get the idea? Open up to playful ways to explore the world around you.

FOLLOW UP: Extending your insights

- Try verbalizing out loud during your observations. (Refer to Goethe's and Whistler's technique presented on page 182 for suggestions.)

- Write about the experience. What ideas and images came to you? What new perspectives or associations did you discover about the subject? How can you use these to address some project you currently face?

- Draw your ideas. Create whatever images or ideas seemed to be interesting.

•Take photographs of the object using your "new eyes." Try focusing through your altering lens and capture the image for later exploration.

•Create music or a dance based upon the new perspectives. Use any other means you feel is appropriate. Kleevision can stimulate many imaginative perceptions of our ordinary, and often too familiar, reality.

COLLAGE CREATION — MAX ERNST, JOAN MIRO, ROBERT RAUSCHENBERG, AND JEAN TINGUELEY

GOAL: To stimulate playful imaginative thinking.

The word *collage* comes from the French verb which means, "to paste." The collage assembles various pictures, either as wholes or in fragments, in such a way that each individual visual element loses its separate identity as it becomes part of the collage. The collage is greater than, and often radically different from, the sum of its parts.

Max Ernst discovered what many children know, that creating a collage stimulates the imagination. Ernst called a collage "the chance encounter of two distant realities." When distant realities (two or more separate pictures or parts of pictures) collide in a collage, the imagination transforms them into an altogether new reality transcendent over the separate elements. For example a picture of a banana may become a boat, a smile, an airplane wing, a totally abstract image, etc. The imagination transforms the meaning ordinarily attached to a banana (a yellow tropical fruit) into a symbol for many different things. If we experience a banana or anything else as a symbol, and not as the item we commonly experience, the imagination finds numerous uses for the symbol in the collage.

Ernst sought to liberate his mind from what he called "ready-made reality," an inadvertent consequence of the logical–rational mindset, by creating collages. Joan Miró, Robert Rauschenberg, and Jean Tingueley also used collages to transform ordinary experiences into new creative expressions. Creating a collage requires that we unbridle the imagination so that it can transform "ready-made reality" into symbolic expressions. For example, the imagination understands that there is more to a banana than just 130 calories of tropical tastiness. The imagination also understands that "banana" includes color, size, shape, texture, lines, form, negative spaces, etc. The imagination uses these and other symbolic elements to construct a collage. The are several ways to create collages:

Variation 1: Ernst's Method

We may construct the collage as a completely random process. Cut out several pictures or parts of pictures that interest you from magazines, newspapers, books, catalogues, etc. Then quickly paste these items together without conscious forethought as to what you are doing or how the final product will look. Be open to your feelings and impressions, and let the collage form itself without any introspection or deliberation. Continue until you have used all the items or until you "feel" that you have completed the collage. Trust your hunches! Record your thoughts and impressions in your journal.

Variation 2: Miró's Method

Gather pictures that interest you as in the above exercise and spread them out before you. Allow your imagination to play with these images so that it creates new perspectives on them, much the same way Leonardo and Klee created new perspectives from everyday reality. "See" in each item more than what we normally see, more than just a banana, for example. Next, imagine how certain items might interrelate, how a banana as an airplane wing might relate to a screwdriver as a fuselage.

Play with the items and move them around. Try several combinations until you get a feeling for possible ways to use these patterns. Form patterns and associations without forcing them. Paste the pictures together using the patterns and associations your imagination has furnished. If new associations develop as you construct the collage, consider incorporating them into the project. Notice how it feels to create something based upon your spontaneous impressions. Continue until your collage feels complete. Finally, record your thoughts and impressions in your journal.

Variation 3: Rauschenberg and Tingueley

The Object Collage — Another collage method uses actual physical objects to form the collage. Metal pipes, salad bowls, pastries, money, dirty socks, empty bottles, spark plugs, etc. can become a collage. Through the collage, Rauschenberg and Tingueley transform objects chosen from modern urban culture into new ways to perceive things we ordinarily take for granted. You may not want to use glue or to weld the objects together as did these artists; instead, you can use modeling clay to hold smaller items together temporarily. You also may want to create collages of larger objects on the floor or table.

Use either Ernst's or Miró's variations to create the object collage. You may want to make a statement with the collage such as your impression of designer clothes or society's preoccupation with "disposable" items, or you may let the collage form without a pre-determined subject.

A CHILD'S EYE–VIEW — TURNER, OLDENBERG, AND DUBUFFET

GOAL: To use the uninhibited expressiveness of young children as a source for the imagination.

The great landscape artist J. M. W. Turner used a technique to stimulate his imagination that can benefit us as well. Turner would visit his friends who had young children and give the youngsters watercolors and paper to make drawings. He gave them no instructions or directions; he just let them draw anything they wanted. Being playful young children whose imaginations had not yet been stifled by logic and rationality, the results were original and spontaneous expressions of primary creativeness.

Turner would then take the drawings, observe them with an open mind, and create his own visual impressions from the children's work, in much the same way Leonardo imagined faces among the stains on the wall. Turner used these visual impressions to inspire his landscape studies. He would add details from his own observations of the countryside to the children's drawings and create new perspectives for the familiar landscape. These studies inspired many of Turner's impressive landscape paintings.

Other great artists have used young children's drawings to generate ideas for their works. Jean Dubuffet and Claes Oldenberg are among those who acknowledge inspiration from children's drawings and artwork. Creativity researcher Howard Gardner explains how children's drawings could be inspirational to adults willing to view them with an open mind. Gardner has observed what he calls the "artful scribbles" of young children and found them to break the rules of convention, style, and form in a manner similar to great artists such as Cézanne, Picasso, Pollock, and others. Artists find inspiration in children's drawings largely because both speak the same language, the language of primary creativeness. This ability is not limited to great artists. It exists for us, if we grant our imagination freedom.

Procedure

You may have young children at home. If not, most likely you have neighbors, friends, or relatives with young children. Children age six or under (children whose creative expressions probably have not yet begun to conform to adults' expectations) will be the best candidates. Regardless of age, if your prospective young artists usually draw pictures to please others, and not for the sheer joy of drawing, you better look elsewhere. Provide various drawing materials and let the children draw whatever they want. Give them no instructions or helpful hints and, most importantly, place no expectations upon their work. Use the following ideas to stimulate your imagination as you study the children's drawings.

1. **Use Turner's method:** Use your imagination as a guide while you observe the drawings. Grant freedom to the imagination to "see" or "feel" anything it desires — either concrete items or abstract impressions — in the drawings. Next, add any details to the children's drawings you feel are necessary to express what your imagination has shown you. Use any media you feel necessary to create your impressions.

2. **Collage Creation:** Cut up the drawings and use them in a collage. Be random as you cut the drawings, just let the scissors guide themselves. Refer to the collage activity above for suggestions on generating inspiration from the collage.

3. **Create your own drawings:** Once your imagination has generated impressions and associations from the children's drawings, create your own drawings based upon these impressions. Use whatever media you feel appropriate.

EXERCISES: KNOW THYSELF & ENHANCING SELF–AWARENESS AND SELF–ACCEPTANCE

"Know Thyself!" was one of Socrates' most frequent admonitions to his students. For, if we do not know ourselves, he proclaimed, then we cannot understand that which is around us. Carl Jung brings Socrates' message into modern terms in his book, *Modern Man in Search of a Soul*. Jung maintains that, since we change and evolve throughout our entire lifetime, our commitment to knowing ourselves, necessarily, must be a lifelong process. This is especially true once we reach what Jung calls "the second half of life." During our early years, we devoted considerable energy to the process of identity formation, the process of discovering our individual uniqueness in a rather conformist world. Once we reach mid–life, however, Jung feels we no longer need these energies to form our self–concept. Instead, we must direct our energy towards redefining ourselves in terms more appropriate for the second half of life. We must separate the fact from the fiction in our self–concept.

In his book, *To Have or To Be*, Erich Fromm maintains that our self-concept, rather than being an objective perspective upon ourselves, is a mixture of certain real properties, such as our knowledge and skills, with certain fictitious properties that we have assumed to be true. These fictitious properties are the "labels" (the names we or others have attached to ourselves: dopey, hyperactive, artistic, silly, chubby, talented, athletic, etc.) that we acquired during our childhood and teenage years. Gradually, through the years and through repeated exposure to these descriptions, they became components of our self-concept. We, most likely, have changed substantially since our earlier years; yet, we often treat these fictitious, acquired labels as if they continued to describe us in the present.

No doubt you can think of several labels that were attached to you in earlier years that still have an impact upon you today. Whether the labels were favorable or unfavorable is not important, according to Jung. He states that if your present self–concept still conforms to these outdated labels and descriptions, you may be preventing your true self from emerging as you mature and evolve. In order to "relabel" ourselves in terms of our present expectations and desires for actualization, we must develop awareness of these labels and transform them into new ways to express "who we are."

— EXERCISES —

SYMBOLS FOR FEELINGS

GOAL: To encourage symbolic expression of our inner feelings and awareness which may be difficult to express verbally.

You probably have had the feeling. You experience intense inner feelings about something, but you cannot find the words to express these feelings adequately. You may become frustrated which further compounds your plight. The primary reason for this difficulty is that our inner, more subjective realms often do not speak the same language as ordinary verbal consciousness. Inner language, because it is primarily unconscious, symbolic, and subjective, has little in common with our more objective, rational outer language. Without a means to unite these two diverse languages, we will encounter numerous occasions when we cannot adequately express our true inner awareness.

One way to bridge the gap between our feelings and the ability to express them is through symbols. Carl Jung believes that "because there are innumerable things beyond the range of human understanding, we constantly use symbolic terms to represent concepts that we cannot fully define or fully comprehend." William Blake expresses the same awareness as he writes: "The essence of life can only be conveyed by the symbol." Each experience we have possesses many important associations which lie outside ordinary conscious awareness.

Symbols relate the larger mass of unconscious information in a way that the usual verbal mode acting on its own cannot. The following activity fosters a link between inner states of awareness and our ordinary waking consciousness by using symbolic expression. This allows us to gather insight from the multitude of unconscious mental activities which might otherwise be inaccessible to ordinary verbal consciousness. The procedure for the activity is as follows:

1. Become aware of any instance in which you cannot find words to express your feelings. If it is convenient at that immediate time, proceed with the activity. If not, make notes for later use. Describe as best as you can the feelings you are experiencing at that moment, remembering that these feelings, even when intense, are extremely short-lived.

2. Describe out loud your feelings as best as you can. It helps to use phrasing similar to, "Now I am feeling..." or "At this moment I am aware of..." This phrasing helps focus our attention upon the present experience and assists in shutting out distractions. As you describe your feelings, pay attention to anything which seems difficult to communicate. Does it pertain to a person, a particular situation, something from the past, a future expectancy, etc? Identify as best as you can what it is that you want to express. *Whatever* ideas come to your mind should be noted without judging or evaluating them. Let your inner feelings surface as they may.

3. Once you feel you have identified the major items needing further expression, begin to include symbolic expression in the process. Take the feelings which are difficult for you to express verbally and create symbols for them. Do not worry about what to create; just start

creating *something*. Taking action, not continuing in ordinary consciousness' deliberation, opens communication channels between inner and outer awareness.

4. Experiment with colors, forms, elements, and shapes that you feel communicate the essence of your feelings. Let the symbols form without conscious planning. Avoid any attempts to evaluate or criticize the symbols you create. The goal is to open channels of communication — not evaluate our artistic abilities. As long as you feel that the symbol expresses feelings which words could not, this purpose has been met.

5. Keep a symbol dictionary or symbol journal to reinforce symbolic thinking. Look for patterns and connections that may appear among your symbols. Notice if some symbols appear often or seem to express inner feelings more accurately. You might even try writing descriptions of your feelings and place a symbol at a point where it could substitute for words. Once you develop symbols for your feelings, try extending your symbol "vocabulary" and use symbols to express other ideas besides feelings.

6. Explore what you have discovered about yourself through this process. How have you increased self–awareness? How can you use this new information? Record these insights in your journal.

A CONSTELLATION OF YOU

GOAL: To use symbolic expression as a means to promote self-awareness.

This activity provides us with an opportunity to "relabel" ourselves in ways that we now find appropriate. It uses symbolic expression as a means to provide us with new, self–determined labels. Creating new ways to perceive

ourselves fosters self–acceptance and promotes attainment of
our highest potential. The procedure is as follows:

1. Become familiar with constellations. Look at them in the
   sky, in books, or in sky charts. Ancient people looked
   at the sky and found an endless assortment of "beings"
   in the heavens. Constellations embodied the aliveness
   sensed in the universe by these ancient civilizations.
   Orion, Pegasus, Taurus, etc. all were important means
   of understanding the universe and our place within it.

2. Develop a constellation that you feel embodies "the real
   you." List the attributes and characteristics that you feel
   most identify you today. Your list may include both
   physical and emotional characteristics. Next, imagine
   how you can create symbols to express these attributes.
   How can you symbolize your tenacity, for example, or
   your sense of humor? What can you discover in looking
   at yourself that can be represented in graphic form?
   Give your imagination free reign. Be open to any ideas
   or impressions that you encounter.

3. Create the constellation. Use your imagination to bring
   it into reality in any form you feel is appropriate.
   Incorporate symbols if necessary. Use whatever materials you need. Create it as a mobile or sculpture if you
   desire.

4. Display the constellation where you can see it often.
   Become conscious of it during the day and explore the
   new ways to express yourself that you have created.
   You may create new constellations if the need arises.
   Creative people thrive upon self–discovery and the
   enhanced self–realization it provides.

5. Record in your journal any new insights that may have
   emerged from this process. Review your notes
   periodically to determine if greater self–awareness has
   changed your self–concept.

WRITING A PERSONAL MYTH

GOAL: To facilitate self–awareness through the creation of a personal myth that uses symbolic expression.

Numerous cultures have developed myths as intricate descriptive accounts of the universe and our place within it. Myths utilize elaborate imagery and symbolism that offer a particular culture's hypotheses about the universe. Myth creation served as a discovery process for these cultures, and it allowed them to express through symbolic imagery their awareness of themselves and the world. Myths have played a vital role in human history, and they still have many effects upon our lives today.

Carl Jung found a rich symbolic vocabulary in myths which can be useful in increasing our self–understanding. His book, *Man and His Symbols*, indicates that symbols are at the heart of the mythical experience, and that both our attitudes and behavior are influenced by symbols, often in ways which lie outside our conscious awareness. Jung and others have employed symbolic imagery from myths as a means to assist self–discovery. Creating a personal myth is a powerful technique for increasing self–understanding.

We also can use the personal myth to help us get in touch with the storehouse of imagery and symbolism that presently affects our attitudes and behaviors. Access to this inner, often unconscious, imagery facilitates creative thinking and self–awareness. As we express our inner imagery through the external process of writing, we nurture self–awareness. The following exercise accomplishes this objective by accessing inner imagery and using it to create a personal myth. The benefits of the activity come from using both your imagination and conscious awareness to explore imagery. Use the following guidelines to stimulate your creative imagination as write your personal myth:

1. Let yourself be the central character; however, use the third person when your character is talking.

2. Visualize yourself as you would like to be in the myth and focus your thoughts on the details such as: your age; your position (wizard, princess, healer, shaman, goddess, farmer, etc.); your clothing; and your lifestyle.

3. Visualize the setting you desire. Imagine the country-side, the buildings, and the time–period. Focus on the sensory details of this setting to enhance imagery and to stimulate your imagination during myth creation.

4. The myth will incubate at both conscious and uncon-scious levels; therefore, allow the setting, other characters, and your own character to flow through your mind for a few days. Consider possible actions they might take and what you would do in various situations. Let the mind explore! Remember, this is a myth, so anything is possible.

5. List symbols you can create that suit the story. Such familiar symbols as flags, banners, religious icons, and coats of arms are a good starting place. Draw, make, or find these symbols to enhance the mythical setting.

6. Begin to write once you develop a "feeling" for the myth. Begin with a description of the setting. Include as many sensory details as possible in the description. Allow the story to emerge on its own. Incorporate the images and impressions created during your visualiza-tion and incubation processes. Continue until you feel the story is complete.

7. Once you have created the myth, explore it just as you would explore a novel. Consider your character and its actions. Were you strong or weak in the face of adversity? How did you interact with other characters? What symbols played major roles? What do these and other questions you might ask yourself reveal? How can you use these revelations to enhance your self–understanding? Record these insights in your journal.

PORTRAIT OF A GOOD DECISION

GOAL: To increase awareness of our decision-making abilities.

1. Create a list of the ten best decisions that you have made. It does not matter how important or far-reaching in impact these decisions were, only that you feel they were successful decisions.

2. Next, on 3 X 5 inch notecards or similar-sized paper, create a symbol or image that represents this decision in your own mind. Create a symbolic or pictorial means to express this decision without concern that it needs to "look like" anything in particular. Be open to any impressions that come to you. For example, if you made a decision to delegate some of your workload to subordinates in the department, thereby freeing yourself for more appropriate functions, you might draw a clock or watch to indicate potentially better time utilization. Or, you could draw a trophy being presented to you by your subordinates because you delegated new functions to them that are a challenge and source of motivation.

3. After you have created images for these decisions on the notecards, arrange them in chronological order from left to right in front of you. The card on the left would be the first event, and the one on the right would be the last. If any of the events are on-going or continuing occurrences, place them in the order at the time they first began. Keep the notecards in a single line.

4. Now begin to explore these events. Look for connections and similarities among the various decisions. What common elements do you see? Are there any patterns to your successful decision making? Are there periods in your life when you made the best decisions? Are you making better decisions now than in the past? What does this tell you?

5. Try reversing the chronological order of these decisions so that the last decision is on your left and the first one is on your right. Again, look for connections and patterns among your decisions. Do any new insights come by viewing them in reverse order?

6. Now that you have two sets of insights about your best decisions, look for connections and relationships between the natural and reversed chronological perspectives. Do any new connections emerge? What can you learn by viewing decisions in this manner? Record your insights in your journal.

7. Now that you have a number of insights about your best decision making in the past, you can use them as a tool in making future decisions. The next time you encounter a problem and need a creative outcome, use the insights you have just generated to assist in decision–making.

Variations

• Use this exercise to explore your best business or career decisions. Compare insights from business and personal decision making. Are there similarities, differences? Explore what these may mean. We often can transfer strategies or operations that operate well for us in one area to our other needs.

• List the ten most creative things you have ever done. Explore the connections among these actions.

• Use the exercise to explore your best interpersonal relationships.

> The goal of self–knowledge is that we will understand the universe more fully as we find our own place within it. We will not be able to understand the universe any better than we understand ourselves.

EXERCISES: NOWNESS — PRESENT TENSE AWARENESS

As mentioned in Part One, Vincent van Gogh strongly believed that losing oneself in the present and being inspired by our immediate surroundings enhances our creative potential. Such complete absorption in an object or experience at hand creates an "encounter" which helps us overcome routine, stereotyped thinking about whatever lies before us. Complete absorption in the present moment also was an important factor in Richard Wagner's creative inspiration. He believed that present tense awareness provided him with "a capacity to saturate all my being unreservedly with my subject which—protected thusly from trivial pursuits—grows in depth and intensity." His insight tells us why we must remain in the present, *to avoid trivial distractions.* Any form of distraction, either internal (our thoughts or bodily sensations) or external (sensory experiences), may disrupt present tense awareness and thwart potential encounters with our experiences.

NOTE: The exercises in this chapter, in addition to fostering present tense awareness, also encourage **mental discipline** which will help you remain centered during meditation activities.

PRELIMINARY EXERCISE FOR PRESENT TENSE AWARENESS

GOAL: To nurture present tense awareness ("mindfulness") of our immediate environment.

1. Make it a part of your daily routine to spend at least five minutes actively exploring an object. Sunsets, flowers, trees, rocks, seashells, and other aspects of nature are

good places to begin. Use the same object for the entire five minutes. To facilitate concentration, find a time and place that are quiet and free of distractions to practice the exercise. If you desire to engage present tense awareness under other conditions, don't be discouraged if your mind wanders a bit at first.

2. Focus your full attention upon the item you have selected. Explore its details using as many of your senses as possible (feel it, smell it, taste it, hear it, as well as see it). Use your senses as your primary means to explore the item and avoid trying to "think" about it. Also, refrain from using your imagination to explore the object (imagining how it might look as a lamp, wondering how it might feel about you, and imagining how it would look if it became larger are examples of imaginative thinking which should be avoided). Stay focused upon your sensory impressions of the object!

3. If your mind begins to wander from your subject, simply refocus it on the subject. This is much like learning to ride a bicycle. At first you had to think about what you were doing. Later you realized this was no longer necessary. Through time, you will learn to stay in the present tense without much difficulty or without even thinking about it. Van Gogh, Wagner, and many other great minds knew present tense encounters with life experiences stimulated their creative potential.

VERBALIZING OUT LOUD — GOETHE AND JAMES WHISTLER

A formidable barrier to developing our innate human potential and becoming more creative is that, in our rush to get ahead in life, we may assume that we already know what we will encounter in the world. If we have a busy schedule and feel that we already know what to expect, then we probably will not take the time to "encounter" our surroundings. Not stopping to smell the roses because we're rushed and already know what roses smell like is an efficient way to move through life. It is not, however, the way to develop our highest mental and spiritual potential.

Fortunately, there are techniques to help us overcome this barrier to developing our human potential. Rosemary Gaymer feels that present tense, highly focused awareness is not a talent reserved only for a few creative souls. Rather, she believes it to be a skill which anyone can learn—*if they will expend the effort.* A primary way to stimulate present tense awareness is to describe out loud any objects or ideas that interest you or seem to have potential merit. Verbalizing your immediate impressions focuses your awareness and facilitates having an encounter with the object or experience.

The great German writer Goethe often used a verbalization technique to generate insights for his writings. He would invite an "imaginary friend" to his house and place an empty chair in the center of the room for his guest. Next, Goethe would pretend that he was describing some new character, setting, or plot to his invisible guest and actually would put his ideas into words. By verbalizing these story elements, Goethe found that he grasped their subtleties and fine points more completely than if he had merely thought about them. Goethe believed that his verbalization technique produced highly imaginative, yet realistic, writing.

James Whistler used a similar verbalization method to develop his artistic expression. Whistler liked to take a friend along on nightly walks along city streets, and, as they strolled along, Whistler would be on the lookout for an interesting scene. When one presented itself, he would study it carefully and would then describe out loud any details about the scene that seemed interesting or unusual. Occasionally, after observation, he would even turn his back to the scene and describe from an observation–sharpened memory what he had just seen. In addition, his friend would give him feedback to enhance his awareness. Whistler called these episodes his "Nocturnal Tone Poems."

Win Wenger's research confirms that verbalization methods similar to those Goethe and Whistler used can contribute to our self–realization efforts. He has found that if we "describe the dickens" out of an object while we observe it, we will more likely "encounter" the object. As we describe an object out loud, initially we will verbalize the familiar, routine terms (pretty, colorful, interesting, spectacular, etc.) that the ordinary waking consciousness uses to describe its awareness. If we continue to describe the object out loud, we soon will run out of these familiar descriptions. At that point —*if we expend the effort to persist* —we likely will transcend an ordinary experience of the object and create an encounter with it. Then, because we have nurtured present tense awareness, even the most ordinary, mundane items can stimulate our minds, just as they stimulated the great minds .

Procedure

1. Initially, select an object in which you have strong interest and place it in front of you. For a minimum of five minutes describe the object **out loud**. Do not judge or censor your thoughts; say whatever comes to mind. In other words, allow your "stream of consciousness" (your immediate, uncensored thoughts and impressions) to emerge. If you run into difficulty—*do not stop*— but continue describing the object out loud. Reaching new perspectives requires that we press onwards when we have reached the limits of ordinary waking con-sciousness. (In jogging, remember, the first mile or so does not provide as much benefit as the last mile).

2. You may wish to describe the object to a partner or tape recorder. This allows you to receive feedback on the experience. Pay attention to the descriptions you use and notice if you shift from the descriptive terms characteristic of ordinary awareness (big, brightly colored, pretty, etc.) to more metaphorical and imaginative descriptions (a pattern resembling a railroad

yard, it smells much like humor would smell, etc.) characteristic of enhanced awareness.

3. When you finish, record in your journal any new insights or perspectives that you may have generated. Describe out loud the same object on different occasions and note any new ideas that may emerge. You may also describe out loud, as did Goethe, any thoughts or ideas that you are evaluating.

HERE AND NOW OF AWARENESS

GOAL: To discover how our attention operates so we can focus it upon present tense awareness.

Imagine for a second that you are in a dark forest at night and have a small flashlight. You hear strange sounds all around, and you want to see what is out there. You hear a sound and quickly turn your flashlight towards it. You see what caused the noise; however, there are other noises coming from places that are not illuminated by the flashlight's beam. Everywhere you turn the light, you see something making noise; yet, you cannot see all the noise–makers at once. You realize that you must choose one particular item to illuminate at any time from the multitude of items around you. There is always "more out there," but you just can't include everything in the light at the same time.

Just as you would choose what to select out of the forest with your flashlight, you choose what is sent into the beam of your conscious flashlight. Unfortunately, many people feel that they have little control over their conscious flashlight because that "little voice" inside their head dictates where their awareness will settle. That little voice is our consciousness, our *ordinary waking consciousness*, that is. Since its logical–rational nature feels most comfortable in the realm of familiar, previously encountered ideas and experiences, it often leads our mind away from new or unfamiliar experiences and steers it towards the "safety" of whatever it already understands. Ordinary waking consciousness sacrifices the ability to nurture potential encounters for the security blanket of the status quo.

If we encounter a new object or life experience and that little voice tells us, "I already understand this, so let's move on to something else" or "I'll think about what a great weekend I had," then we will thwart present–centered awareness. Without occasionally asserting our need for new encounters, we will be held captive to those things that little voice already understands. We must learn to direct our awareness towards our immediate experiences—even if the little voice tells us, "Oh I already fully understand that, so let's look elsewhere."

Marilyn Ferguson's book, *The Aquarian Conspiracy*, tells us how to transcend the shackles of ordinary waking consciousness. She states that all we need to do is *pay attention to the flow of attention itself.* In other words, we must learn how we focus our own minds upon our life experiences. We must observe our own mind in operation and discover what it chooses, and what it does not choose, to include in awareness at any moment. Knowing how we "pay attention" to our experiences will help us nurture present–centered awareness. It also will help reduce our "little voice's" paranoia about new or unfamiliar experiences.

Psychologist Frederick Perls maintains that we can develop substantial control over our attention–focusing ability by making efforts to stay in what he calls "the present continuum of awareness." Perls, like Ferguson, realizes that we alone are responsible for the current contents of our awareness, because we alone have created our ordinary waking consciousness. We *choose* what to cast into the consciousness spotlight from the plethora of items around us. Likewise, we alone are responsible for changing the contents of our awareness, if we perceive such a need. The following exercise helps focus our attention upon the present continuum of awareness.

Preliminary Considerations: The goal for the exercise is to discover the ebb and flow of your own attention. Find a quiet place to perform the activity. Later, as you feel comfortable, expand the setting for the exercise so that you can use it whenever you feel the need or the desire.

1. Take a few moments to relax your body and mind before you begin. During the exercise, DO NOT stop to evaluate or judge any aspect of it until you are completely finished. If you stop to evaluate or criticize, you exit immediately from the present continuum of awareness and re–enter ordinary waking consciousness.

2. Create sentences that express whatever is on your mind *at that very moment.* (Note: this activity also uses our "stream of consciousness" to promote centered awareness.) Let each sentence begin with phrasing similar to: "Now I'm aware that...", "At this moment I'm aware of...", etc. Complete the sentence with any impression or observation that is on you mind. Do not worry if it sounds foolish or trivial. If you are aware of it, then it is in your conscious awareness and should be expressed! Phrasing the contents of your awareness in this manner activates the present continuum of awareness. State your sentences out loud — don't just think about them. Close your eyes, if you like.

Examples of present tense awareness:

•At this moment I hear a truck passing.

•Now I'm aware of the smell of peanut butter.

•Now I feel a burst of Spring entering my room.

•At this moment I am thinking about the weather.

•Right now I'm thinking about what homeless people do during thunderstorms.

•Now I am aware of being hungry.

3. Continue to verbalize the contents of your awareness for at least three minutes. After paying attention to the flow

of your attention, relax for a moment and then explore (writing, drawing, etc.) what your awareness has just shown you. Also explore your awareness by asking yourself these or similar questions: Was I more aware of internal stimuli (inner physiological sensations, mental images, feelings, etc.) or external stimuli (sensory perceptions)? How did it feel to follow the flow of my awareness? When did I feel the most (or least) comfortable during the exercise? What new insights or awareness did this exercise create?

4. Perform the exercise daily for a few weeks and keep a journal of your observations. Pay attention to any recurring thoughts, sensations, or feelings. You may find sources of hidden interest if certain items reappear in your continuum of awareness. Likewise, if you encounter any negative imagery, make notes in your journal. Reflect upon changes in your attention–focusing ability.

NOTE: You may use the following exercise to promote a disciplined mind **during Step Two** of the meditation process described in the next chapter.

BEACH SAND WRITING

GOAL: To enhance present–centered awareness through an extended visualization.

Many great composers such as Mozart, Beethoven, and Brahms would let the entire score of a new composition flow into their awareness as a stream of images and impressions. Likewise, Einstein found he could let the steps in new equations he was testing flow into his awareness in a streamlike fashion. Other great minds report a similar ability to encounter creative inspiration during present–centered awareness. The following activity enables us to develop a stream of mental images which will encourage present–

centered awareness. Note: If you are not using this activity as part of a meditation session, relax for a few moments before you begin.

Variation 1: Numbers

1. Imagine that it is a beautiful, warm day and you are at a beach by the edge of the water where the sand is moist and densely packed. Use your imagination to create a clear mental image of this scene by focusing upon sensory details (*seeing* sea gulls flying overhead, *smelling* the salty air, *feeling* the sand's grittiness, etc.) you might expect at the beach. Next, imagine writing in the soft, moist sand with your finger. Imagine how the sand would feel as you pull your finger through it. Feel the sand puckering up around your finger as you pull your finger through it. Focus on that sensation for a moment.

2. Now imagine beginning to write a series of numbers in the sand. Start with the number "1" and slowly write it in the sand in front of you. *Pay attention to the sensations created by pulling your finger through the sand.* After you draw the number, imagine a wave slowly coming in, covering the number, and washing the number away as the wave retreats. Now slowly draw the number "2" and again watch the wave come and wash the number away. "Adjust" the speed of the waves, if you like, until they feel comfortable. Continue this process all the way through the number "10." If your mind starts to drift during the drawing, do not worry. Simply refocus your mind upon drawing the numbers in the sand and continue with the activity. With practice, the mind learns to follow a series of inner images just as proficiently as it will follow a series of sensory impressions in outer awareness.

Variation 2: Alphabet

Repeat the above exercise substituting the letters of the alphabet for numbers. As this will require a longer series of images, you first should feel comfortable with the above series. If your mind wanders, simply refocus it upon drawing the alphabet.

Variation 3. Drawings

The above exercises focus upon drawing concrete forms such as numbers and letters. In this variation, however, you may draw anything that you like in the sand. Your may draw either something tangible (a palace, clown, airplane, picture of yourself, etc.) or something more abstract (your impression of Mozart's music, how you feel about working on weekends, how you feel about being late for meetings, etc.). Focus your full attention upon transferring whatever image is on your mind into a drawing in the sand. "Draw" it in as complete detail as possible. If your mind wanders, simply refocus it upon the drawing.

CREATING AFFIRMATIONS

Research shows that neural messages tend to flow along familiar roads, along paths of least resistance. If a neural pathway is traversed over and over, it becomes a well-worn footpath.

Judith Hooper & Dick Teresi, *The 3-Pound Universe*

GOAL: To create affirmations to center our minds and nurture positive mental activities.

Remember, our hands alone operate the control panel of conscious awareness. We *choose* what enters into consciousness and what does not. Many people feel trapped in the never-ending and never-satisfying cycle of wistfully replaying their past or hopefully constructing their future. Dwelling upon our past or our future not only thwarts present–centered awareness, but it also causes us to become like the disconsolate character, Billy Pilgrim, in Kurt Vonnegut's *Slaughterhouse Five*. Pilgrim, not satisfied with life as it is, becomes "unstuck in time" and loses his ability to stay in the present tense of his life. His inability to remain in contact with his immediate life experiences ultimately leads him along an endless path of isolation and confusion. If we, like poor Billy, center our attention upon our past in hopes of "improving" or "reliving" it in our minds, or if we allow ourselves to dwell upon the future because "it just has to be better," then we miss the opportunity to benefit from the present moment. Frederick Perls feels that habitual introspection about either the past or the future can produce damaging effects to our psychological well-being, because introspection reinforces avoiding, rather than confronting, life's challenges. To escape the present for the perceived safety of either the past or the future will thwart our self–realization. We cannot improve ourselves in either the past or the future—only in the infinite _NOW_. To avoid habitual introspection about the past or future we need the unlimited power of affirmations.

It is not enough just to say, "I don't want to think about the past or the future," and try to turn our attention back to the present. In, _The Global Brain_, Peter Russell tells us why this method often fails: "Our self-model cannot be changed by thinking, by argument, by analysis, or by simply deciding to change it, since it is the frame of reference that underlies all thought, argument analysis, and decision making, and as such is beyond their scope." In other words, we must change our mental framework itself, _not just the products of the framework_, if we are to experience present–centered awareness. Affirmations help replace the foundation of past or future–oriented thinking with present–centered awareness, a mental framework substantially more suitable for self–realization activities. Remember, if our thoughts run along a well-worn neural pathway, then we must take steps to create new pathways. That is the role of affirmations.

The Power Behind Affirmations

Samskara — the ancient Hindu concept that thoughts repeated over and over accumulate energy in the mind and help build our character. *Whatever* we repeat to ourselves, through time, becomes our reality. Positive thoughts become positive realities, while negative thoughts create negative realities.

"Possibility Thinking" — Another power source for affirmations is a belief in their possibility. J. A. Hadfield believes that suggesting affirmative ideas to ourselves does not make us believe something to be true when it really is not. *It means making something true by believing in its possibility.* When we use affirmations, what we hold in our minds as being reality in principle becomes our reality in operation. Shakti Gawain concurs with Hadfield's observation in her book, *Creative Visualization.* She maintains that affirmations are strong, positive statements indicating that something already exists. We do not have to "wish" for them, because the mind perceives them as *already* being true.

Affirmations contribute positive, present–oriented energy to all our mental activities. They can be used during relaxation or meditation exercises, at various times during the day, or whenever you feel the need to devote present–centered, positive energy to something you desire. Affirmations also are an excellent way to dispel negative thoughts from our awareness. If you encounter negative thoughts or ideas, then you can replace them quickly with the positive energy found in affirmations. Let's summarize what we know about affirmations:

1. Affirmations are strong positive statements indicating that something already exists, in the *now*. If repeated, the mind accepts them as reality.

2. Affirmations work best if:
   •phrased in the present tense
   •phrased in positive terms
   •phrased as short, clear statements

3. Affirmations may be spoken out loud, written on note-cards and posted where you will encounter them frequently, or repeated silently to yourself.

4. Affirmations can be used during relaxation or meditation or anytime during the day.

Sample Affirmations

•I am centered in the present moment of my life.

•I am relaxed and aware of my feelings.

•I am loved and love others.

•I make good choices about my future.

•Each day I am more creative.

•I have everything I need for making me happy.

•This day is filled with creative possibilities.

•The spirit of the universe fills me with love for all creation.

NOTE: You also may use affirmations after **Step Two** in the meditation process described in the next chapter. Affirmations, if we repeat them to ourselves when we are relaxed, are powerful techniques for creating a more positive and mindful approach to life.

EXERCISES: MEDITATION AND VISUALIZATION

What is Meditation?

Meditation is an activity in which people can expand their awareness in a step–by–step manner. In both Eastern and Western cultures, many people have used the expanded awareness that meditation produces to develop their full mental and spiritual potential. For our purposes, meditation will mean a distinct period of no less than 15 minutes when we will quiet our minds and concentrate our full attention within ourselves to seek inspiration, insight, or union with the universal mind.

Why Meditate?

Consider these ideas for a few minutes:

People who practice meditation undergo shifts in consciousness. Studies suggest that 18 major changes in consciousness occur as one advances in meditation practice. These 18 changes can be broken down into three primary groups of practice—the preliminary practices, the concentrative practices, and the insight (receptive) practices. One who makes it through all three stages experiences a permanent change in perception known as *enlightenment.*

Dr. Daniel Brown, *Transformations of Consciousness in Meditation*

Researchers using EEG monitoring found that people during meditation have increased coherence of alpha and theta brainwave frequencies between the left and right hemispheres of the brain. This synchronization of the brain hemispheres makes creative thinking more likely, because it is much easier to process information and promote innovative perspectives. This is "cognitive receptivity"—the brain is receptive to creative new views of the world.

Dr. Herbert Benson, *Your Maximum Mind*

Researchers trained groups of business leaders in meditation and relaxation skills to measure the impact upon problem-solving abilities. The meditators, compared with control groups who were not taught to meditate, demonstrated the following advantages:

1. They solved problems faster.

2. They felt less tension during problem-solving.

3. They used less mental energy to solve problems.

4. They experienced greater teamwork.

Dr. H.S. Kindler, *The Influence of Meditation upon Group Problem-Solving*

Summary: Benefits of Meditation

1. increased creativity
2. improved problem-solving
3. improved self-discipline
4. fewer negative thoughts
5. overcoming fears
6. improved self-concept
7. physiological benefits
8. greater spiritual awareness

Dr. Herbert Benson, *Your Maximum Mind*

Why do *You* Want to Meditate?

Take a few minutes to reflect upon the information above and also refer back to the reasons why great minds meditated, if you like. Then list your initial thoughts and impressions about meditating before continuing. Reflect upon why you should devote your time and effort to learning how to meditate.

We will focus upon the Four Step Meditation Method. This method combines several powerful Eastern and Western meditation practices, and it offers both beginning

THE FOUR STEPS OF MEDITATION

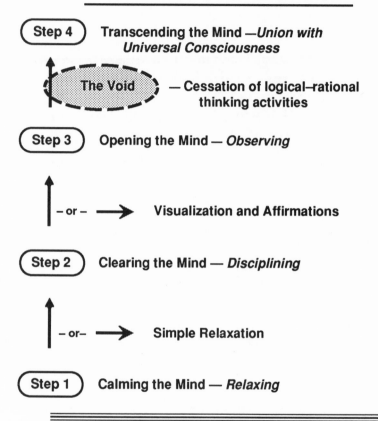

Step 4 Transcending the Mind —*Union with Universal Consciousness*

The Void — Cessation of logical–rational thinking activities

Step 3 Opening the Mind — *Observing*

– or – → **Visualization and Affirmations**

Step 2 Clearing the Mind — *Disciplining*

– or– → **Simple Relaxation**

Step 1 Calming the Mind — *Relaxing*

There are four steps in our union of Eastern and Western meditation practices. Each step leads to a distinct state of consciousness that is conducive to specific activities along the meditative path. Before each meditation session, we should determine our goal for that session. If our goal for a meditation session is one of these alternate activities, then we should depart from the model at the appropriate point as indicated above. For simple relaxation, we would depart after Step 1. For visualization or affirmation activities, depart after Step 2. Remember, please be patient as you develop meditative consciousness.

and more experienced meditators an opportunity to develop and enhance meditative awareness. It also facilitates related activities such as visualization and the use of affirmations. Before proceeding with the techniques themselves, become familiar with the Four Step Method and the choices you may make before each meditative session. It is advisable to decide your purpose for a particular meditation session before you begin. This helps you avoid any unnecessary deliberation while you are in the relaxed, meditative states of awareness.

STEP ONE: CALMING THE MIND — RELAXATION TECHNIQUES

GOAL: To prepare for meditation by slowing the mind down from its usual pace maintained during ordinary waking consciousness.

The technique of resting the mind and the power of dismissing from it all care and worry is probably one of the secrets of energy in all great people.

J. A. Hadfield

The ability to relax the body and mind from its normal attentiveness to internal and external stimuli and to our thought processes is an important first step in meditation. Studies by Dr. Herbert Benson and others have demonstrated numerous effects of relaxation techniques upon the body and mind. Benson indicates that once we relax our mind, it pays less attention to potential distractions and demonstrates greater potential for meditative awareness. His work also indicated that the routine inner dialogue of our ordinary waking consciousness interferes with meditation. We must realize that ordinary waking consciousness' tendency to evaluate, judge, and categorize our experiences is a formidable barrier to achieving the inner calmness needed during meditation. There are, however, factors that facilitate relaxation including the ones listed below.

Factors Enhancing Relaxation

A quiet environment — this reduces the mind's natural efforts to "danger–scan" any sounds it picks up. This learned response serves to protect us from potential dangers by alerting us and then prompting us to focus attention upon the source of the sound to determine if there is an imminent danger. A quiet environment helps reduce this potential distraction to relaxation. Also, direct your telephone calls to an answering machine or switch off the ringing mechanism to avoid this potential interruption.

A passive attitude — it would be counter-productive if our efforts to induce relaxation would themselves become a source of tension. The key to maintaining a passive attitude is to hold no preconceived ideas about how you *should* feel. Each meditation session is a unique experience; therefore, there is no "right" meditative experience. You may find it helpful to avoid forcing your thoughts in any particular direction or holding on to any particular sensation or thought that you experience during the session. Through time and patience you will begin to notice that your thoughts slow down on their own.

A comfortable position — one in which the body feels no particular physical stress. In most cases, sitting in a comfortable chair with your feet on the floor is best. Your arms can either be in your lap, by your side, or placed upon the chair arms. Move yourself around to find a position so that you feel like an "old rag doll"—loose and relaxed. Some people meditate while laying upon their backs. You also may use this position, provided you do not fall asleep often.

"Seating Practices" — specific actions to promote a sense of significance for the meditative session. Eastern meditation practices, as well as many Western religious rituals, place considerable importance upon the *spiritual atmosphere* that is conducive for meditation and contemplation. Creating an environment—both a physical and a mental environment—conducive to meditation helps us recognize and appreciate the importance of meditation in our lives. This facilitates the transition from ordinary daily activities to meditative states of awareness and helps us maintain those states once we experience them. Factors useful in creating the spiritual atmosphere include:

• *The meditation sanctuary* Reserve a special location for meditation or other activities such as reading related to spiritual matters. This will be your primary meditative sanctuary, although other places also can become your sanctuary.

• *Create an environment conducive to meditation.* Use art, pictures, sounds, smells, colors, etc. that you find promote a sense of reverence.

• *Daily meditation* One of the most important seating practices is to treat meditation as a special, yet daily, activity. Have a regular time for your primary meditation session and let nothing interfere with it. Of course you may meditate more than once a day, but at least one session should be a more reverent meditation session.

THREE DEEP BREATHS

GOAL: To develop a "trigger" that will facilitate entry into meditative awareness.

One of the most remarkable things about the human brain is that it can learn to respond to experiences that it frequently encounters without having to *think* about responding. For example, we have encountered stop signs in our driving to such an extent that we no longer have to think: "There is a stop sign. I must place my right foot on the brake petal and stop the car." Instead, we simply stop the car without devoting conscious attention to the process, because the sign has triggered a response. We will use the brain's ability to respond to frequently encountered experiences to our advantage in the meditation process with an activity known as Three Deep Breaths.

PLEASE NOTE: This is a preliminary activity for all meditation sessions

1. Once you have "seated" yourself according to the suggestions above, close your eyes and relax for a minute. Just let the mind and body relax without paying attention to any particular thought or sensation.

2. Next, **slowly** inhale through your nose. Continue to inhale slowly and pay attention to the air as it comes into your nostrils. Focus your full attention to the air as it enters. Feel the air filling your lungs and feel your chest expanding as you continue to fill your lungs to a full, but comfortable level. You also may notice that your shoulders rise slightly as you fill your lungs with air. Once your lungs are full, hold your breath for a moment. Do not hold it until it becomes uncomfortable, just until you have felt the fullness of your lungs for a few moments.

3. Now **slowly** let the air pass from your lungs out through slightly parted lips. Feel the air as it leaves your lungs and feel it passing out through your lips. Also, pay attention to how your shoulders may be lowering themselves and how you may feel as if you were sinking down into the chair. Continue to let the air out slowly until you feel you have emptied your lungs of air. Then pull in your stomach muscles slightly and push out a little more air. Feel it leaving your lungs.

4. Once you have pushed all the air out of your lungs, repeat the cycle. Inhale slowly, hold it (a little longer this time), and let it out completely. Pay full attention to the sensations of breathing in this manner as you complete the cycle. Once you have completed the second deep breath cycle, repeat for one more cycle.

5. After finishing the third deep breath, keep your eyes closed and enjoy the sensations you experience for a minute or two. Let your mind follow your breathing as it returns to its ordinary pace. Just relax for a while before continuing with the meditation session.

6. Through time, you will have developed the Three Deep Breaths as your "trigger" to relax. Then you will notice that simply taking the three breaths will ease you into a state in which your mind and body are very relaxed. Until that time, however, you most likely will need to perform an additional relaxation activity such as the Relaxing Image which follows.

How will I know if I'm relaxed?

The answer to this question varies considerably, as each of us has a different understanding and experience of relaxation. For our purposes, relaxation is a state in which you might notice:

• that there is a reduced need to shift the body in order to feel comfortable

• that the mind does not "race" but seems to "flow" gently from sensation to sensation

• that you rarely, if at all, become concerned with noises or other external sensations

• that your perception of time seems to slow down or disappear; time becomes "irrelevant"

If you feel that you are relaxed, then either proceed to Step Two or return to your daily activities using the procedure for departing relaxed states of awareness presented at the conclusion of the Relaxing Image technique. If you feel that you are not relaxed, then use the following exercise to deepen your relaxation. Be patient. Learning to relax takes time and practice. If your session progresses no further than your experiencing a light degree of relaxation, be thankful! Even a slight departure from the day's routine and tension will benefit you.

THE RELAXING IMAGE

GOAL: To create a multi-sensory mental image to promote deeper relaxation.

If after the Three Deep Breaths you do not feel adequately relaxed, then use the Relaxing Image to deepen your relaxation. Continue to keep your eyes shut and avoid moving your body as much as possible. Allow the image to form in your mind without forcing it or expecting to experience it in any certain manner.

1. Imagine a setting in which you might find yourself relaxed just by being there. Allow the image to form in your mind without forcing it. Once an image appears, begin to add sensory details to enhance its clarity. Adding sensory details to a mental image strengthens the image in our "mind's eye" and helps the mind focus more upon it than upon our present setting and its potential distractions. As you are using your imagination, it really does not matter if you have ever been to a particular setting to create a relaxing image based upon that setting. The imagination's only limits are those you *choose* to set. Suggestions for relaxing images and accompanying multi–sensory details include:

Setting	Multi–sensory Details
a country meadow	• smell of grass or flowers
	• sound of birds chirping or singing
	• sight of white, puffy clouds in a deep blue sky
	• texture of the grass or other objects

porch of a mountain cabin

- sight of a beautiful vista
- smell of cedar trees and clean, fresh air
- texture of the cabin's wood
- sound of the wind whistling in the trees

at the beach

- sound of the waves, sea gulls, seashells
- smell of the salty air
- sight of sailboats gliding upon the water
- texture of the sand or a seashell

a "safe haven" — anyplace that makes you feel comfortable and relaxed—create the multi-sensory details of your "safe haven"

2. Once you have created your image and have begun to experience the setting in a multi-sensory fashion, just relax for a few minutes. Your mind, by providing multi-sensory details to it, will respond to the image as if you were really there, enjoying the relaxation of that setting. Continue to experience the image until you feel very relaxed (refer to the suggestions above for determining relaxation). If your mind wanders off to other images or thoughts, simply let those impressions go as soon as you are aware of their presence. Then refocus upon the relaxing image. Your mind may wander quite frequently at first; however, with ample practice and patience, you will find that it will remain centered upon the relaxing image for an extended period of time.

3. Once you feel very relaxed, you have several options:

  • to continue relaxing either by remaining in the relaxing image or by sitting quietly with your eyes closed and your mind focused upon no particular thoughts

  • to move on to Step Two in the Four Step Meditation Method

  • to prepare for sleep

  • to return to your daily activities (see note below)

Procedure for leaving relaxed or meditative states of awareness

Entry into relaxed or meditative states of awareness is a gradual process involving several steps. Likewise, departing from these states and returning to active waking consciousness also must be a gradual, step–by–step process. This will help you retain the benefits (your relaxation, the insights you received, or your increased self–awareness) you have obtained during the meditative session. When you feel that it is time to return to normal waking consciousness, prepare to leave meditative awareness in the following steps:

1. Silently count backwards from the number five to the number one in a slow, rhythmic manner. When you reach the number one, silently repeat the following or a similar expression: "I am refreshed, relaxed, and mentally alert." When you complete the expression, slowly open your eyes.

2. Draw in a slow, deep breath through your nostrils and then exhale it as if it were a big sigh. Move your feet around a bit and then stretch your arms if you like.

3. If appropriate, record in your journal any impressions or insights you have gleaned from your meditative experience before returning to other activities.

STEP TWO: CLEARING THE MIND WITH DISCIPLINING TECHNIQUES

GOAL: From the *Bhagavadgita* — "To hold the senses and imagination in check and to keep the mind concentrated upon its object."

The mind is flighty and elusive, moving wherever it pleases. Taming it is wonderful indeed, for a disciplined mind invites true joy.

Buddha, *Dhammapada*

The faculty of voluntarily bringing back a wandering attention over and over again is at the very root of judgment, character, and will. No one is *compos sui* if he does not have it. An education which improves this faculty would be an education par excellence.

William James, *Principles of Psychology*

DISCIPLINING METHODS PRIMARILY USED *DURING* MEDITATION SESSIONS

• Open Eye Contemplation

Paul Cézanne maintained that "observation modifies vision." His insight confirms what experienced meditators from Eastern and Western civilizations have known for thousands of years—*that the very act of seeing alters how we see.* Long before Cézanne used the principle of disciplined observation to help art transcend to new levels of expression, Christian mystic St. Teresa of Avila used this principle to teach her students how to obtain the mental discipline necessary for meditation. She wrote, "I do not require of you to form great and serious considerations in your thinking. I require of you only to look." Her method correlates with open eye contemplation methods that Zen masters have used for centuries to teach their students how to control and discipline the mind.

Open eye contemplation of an object is an excellent method to discipline a *relaxed* mind. If you have not relaxed before attempting to discipline the mind, expect a most formidable challenge. Ordinary waking consciousness, as William James indicates, tends to wander, and it must be "educated" by repeatedly returning it to a chosen path. To attempt this task with an unrelaxed mind will create frustration and tension, conditions that thwart meditative awareness. Open eye contemplation, because it places the mind upon a single path to tread, provides sufficient discipline to attain higher meditative states.

1. Select an object for observation. Start with natural objects that will fit comfortably in your hand such as a rock, twig, seashell, piece of bark, etc. Take into consideration that you will need to use the same object *daily* for at least two weeks. Staying with the same object for several weeks enhances mental discipline. You will need to practice the exercise for a minimum of five minutes during the first few weeks and later expand to ten or fifteen minutes to attain the greater discipline required by advanced meditative states.

2. Relax using the exercises and suggestions in Step One. After attaining a state of relaxation, place the object in your hand. Hold it in front of you at a comfortable distance from your eyes. Observe and explore it as a child would, with natural curiosity that is free from any preconceived ideas and judgments. Become fascinated with the object and bring yourself into an intimate relationship with it. Avoid *thinking* about the object: where it came from, how it might look as a piece of jewelry, how much it weighs, how pretty it is, etc. as much as is possible. The goal is to develop a focused mind that is as free from all thought as is possible. Remember we just want to *experience* the object.

3. If your mind starts to wander away from observation or begins to *think* about the object or anything else, simply return to *experiencing* the object. Do not scold yourself for drifting away, simply note that you have drifted and promptly return your mind to the object you are contemplating.

4. Once you feel your mind stays with the object for five minutes with very few wanderings or deliberations about it, expand the time to ten minutes. Once you achieve proficiency at this longer time period, change to a new object and explore it for ten minutes. If you experience difficulty, cut the time back to five minutes and work back up to ten.

5. Once you achieve proficiency with objects found in nature, experiment with other objects such as a simple line drawing, religious image, manufactured item, etc. These require more concentration than you might think, so save them until you are quite proficient with simple natural objects.

• Counting Breaths

Counting your out breaths or exhalations is a method for disciplining the mind used for several thousand years in many cultures. For example, Zen masters have used breathing exercises to help their students overcome the distractions to meditation so often generated by the verbal, conscious mind. When students report distractions, especially imagery of an alluring nature which leads away from proper disciplining of the mind, the masters tell their students: "If you concentrate upon your breathing, distractions will go away."

Counting breaths is simple and easy to learn, yet it is one of the most powerful and effective methods available to help us overcome the distractions of our ordinary consciousness. The goal is to experience—to become one with—your own breathing by counting each exhalation. You simply pay full attention to the counting process and direct attention away from thoughts, sensations, feelings, and other distractions. If your mind strays from counting, gently return it to the counting process.

1. After attaining a relaxed state, sit in a comfortable, erect position. Initially devote five minutes to practicing this technique after your relaxing activities. Continue to practice it during each meditation session until you are able to complete five to ten minutes with minimal distractions.

2. Close your eyes and begin to breathe in full, deep breaths in and out through your nose. Let a slow, natural rhythm develop before you begin to count. *Feel* the air coming in and going out. Pay full attention to your breathing process. Once you feel a rhythm, begin counting each exhalation.

3. Count each separate exhalation until you get to four. Once you have exhaled four times and have reached a count of four, start over at one. Continue counting in the cycle up to four for the duration of the session. If your mind strays, do not worry. Simply return to the counting at either the number you last remember or at one. Also, try to maintain the natural rhythm you established before beginning the counting process. Varying the rhythm is a source of distraction. Remember:*Experience your breathing*!

• Following Sounds

Another way to discipline the mind is through your sense of hearing. This method requires certain devices or instruments to produce sounds that your mind can follow as a way to encourage mental discipline. Your goal is to listen fully and attentively to the sound and keep your mind focused upon it. Experience and explore the sound with an open mind so that you become one with it as in the exercise above. If your mind drifts away, simply refocus upon the sound and continue. You may want to close your eyes to concentrate upon the sound. Practice following sounds for five minutes at first and later increase to ten minutes. Sounds which promote mental discipline include:

Metronome: Select a rate and follow the sound for five to ten minutes.

Tuning fork: Strike the tuning fork (or have someone strike it) and follow the sound until it is completely inaudible. Explore the sounds fully and completely, remembering to avoid thinking about the sounds as much as possible. Repeat the process for about ten minutes.

Wind chimes: If you can attain a relaxed state outdoors, sit in it in a location where you will hear the sound of wind chimes. Follow the sounds produced by the chimes with your full attention.

Chanting: More than likely you will have to use taped chanting. Either Gregorian or Eastern chanting will work if you keep your mind focused upon the sounds of the voices. Do not try to figure out what is being chanted; just stay with the sounds.

• Mandala

The mandala (**mán** da la) is another ancient tool to promote mental discipline. Carl Jung describes the mandala as an archetypal image appearing throughout the human experience. It signifies the wholeness of the self, the wholeness of the psychic ground, and the divinity incarnate in humans. The mandala promotes mental discipline by diverting attention away from the mind's natural verbal chatter by giving it a visual stimulus for observation. The mandala, because it is a powerful symbol of wholeness and unity, helps us discipline the mind while we experience a holistic framework for our meditation.

Jung's book, *Man and His Symbols*, contains many excellent mandalas. Other books containing mandalas are available in bookstores with large selections of books on meditation and Eastern religions. In addition, many people create their own mandalas using paints, pens, colors, and other materials. Another source, particularly important in Western religious practices, is the large, round stained-glass windows found in many cathedrals. You can take a photograph (use daylight film as the illumination source is the sun) from inside the cathedral and get striking results. Experiment until you find several mandalas with which you are comfortable. Using mandalas for disciplining the mind is similar to the open eye observation method.

1. Observe the mandala as you observed objects in the open eye method—become one with it without *thinking* about it. Experience it without trying to attach any particular meaning or impressions to the imagery or symbols within it. Continue for at least five minutes.

2. One way to discipline the mind is to gaze around the mandala in a clockwise fashion. Keep your eyes moving clockwise along the outer edge and then slowly move your line of observation in towards the center of the mandala. After reaching the center, reverse and spiral counter-clockwise out towards the edge. Continue the slow spiraling for the duration of the session.

• Heartbeat

This disciplining technique focuses attention upon one of our many natural rhythms—the heartbeat. The heart provides us with an "inner metronome" that we can use to promote discipline during meditation. As you sit quietly after relaxing the mind, direct your attention inwards to your heartbeat. Concentrate your awareness upon this inner rhythm and let all other sensations pass away. Become one with this inner rhythm.

If you have difficulty locating your heartbeat among the myriad internal sensations, place your fingers upon your wrist as medical personnel do to locate your pulse. Feel the pulsing rhythm with your fingers and let it stimulate awareness of your heartbeat. Focus your full attention on the sensations produced by your heart. Pay attention to this rhythm for a few minutes to enhance mental discipline.

PLEASE NOTE : Any of the above techniques may be practiced at times other than during meditation to enhance mental discipline both for meditation and other activities. Find the particular techniques that seem to work best for you. Additional techniques follow that you can use outside your regular meditation sessions to promote discipline.

DISCIPLINING METHODS TO USE AT TIMES *OTHER THAN DURING* MEDITATION

We can enhance mental discipline during meditation sessions substantially through the inclusion of a few disciplining techniques in our other daily activities. We can hardly discipline our often unruly and distracting mind effectively if we attempt to do so only during meditation sessions. Generating sufficient discipline to calm the mind during meditation requires more frequent attention. Not only will disciplining activities performed as part of our daily life enhance mental discipline during meditation, but it also will assist us in our other daily activities.

If you ever have found your mind wandering during problem-solving, reading, conversation, watching a movie, or other activities, then you most likely are aware of the need to provide yourself with more mental discipline. Developing mental discipline is an investment in ourselves. This investment will pay off both during meditation and your other daily activities, because our minds will be focused fully and completely upon our tasks and problem–solving activities. Enhanced mental discipline, therefore, will increase your overall productivity and effectiveness. We nurture mental discipline simply by adding a few easily practiced techniques to our daily schedule.

• "Washing the Dishes to Wash the Dishes"

Eastern master Thich Nhat Hanh teaches his pupils the value of developing mindfulness as they perform their ordinary activities. He gives them the example of "washing the dishes to wash the dishes." Because most of us see little value in thinking about washing dishes, we disengage our minds from the process of washing dishes and may think about something completely different: the book we are reading, a past experience in which we acted improperly, a problem we face at the office, or a host of other potential distractions from the present moment. We avoid the present experience and hope that something else we could think about will help us tolerate the drudgery of the present task.

If letting our minds wander in this manner were only an occasional response to such activities, we might not need to develop our mental discipline through meditative techniques. Unfortunately, because we seldom realize how easily our minds flee from our daily activities and escape to other activities, we nurture a wandering mind, not mental discipline. It does not matter whether our minds flee to "desirable" thoughts (solving problems, recalling special moments, etc.) or "undesirable" thoughts (our past failures, problems we cannot seem to solve, etc.), because we have encouraged an undisciplined mind in both instances. If we desire to encourage a disciplined mind, then we must devote conscious effort to "washing the dishes to wash the dishes." We must learn to stay centered upon our present experiences, no matter how mundane or unchallenging we may perceive them to be.

We can nurture a more disciplined mind by becoming mindful as we perform a few of our daily tasks or activities. We each have numerous tasks that we must perform as part of our routine. These tasks will provide an excellent opportunity for disciplining our minds and staying centered in the present experience. Use the following guidelines to help you cultivate a more disciplined mind as you perform tasks that are already upon your agenda.

1. Select an activity that you frequently must perform and in which you ordinarily let your mind wander as you perform it. Also, it helps to select one that does not take more than a few minutes to perform until you have had experience with disciplining the mind in this manner. Once you have developed a degree of discipline during shorter tasks, move on to longer tasks such as attentive driving and conscious eating, descriptions of which are below. Examples of such activities might be:

   - washing the dishes
   - brushing your teeth
   - taking a shower
   - waiting in line
   - taking out the trash

   - changing the kitty litter
   - filling the car with gas
   - peeling vegetables
   - brushing your hair
   - waiting for someone

2. As you perform the activity, devote your full attention to the activity. Focus upon the physical sensations you experience, the bodily actions you are using, the steps you must take to perform the activity, and any other elements that directly connect with the experience. Become one with the activity, as if there was nothing else in the whole universe except you and this activity.

3. If any thoughts other than those directly related to your activity creep in, let them go as soon as you have become aware of them. If you follow them any longer than your first awareness of them, then you will have reinforced a wandering mind. As soon as you have let go of a distracting thought, simply return your awareness to performing the activity. Repeat this process each time you encounter a thought that would distract you from mindful awareness.

4. Once you have finished the activity, note your immediate sensations and impressions. Record them in your journal, if you like. Through time, you probably will discover that you have improved your mental discipline by becoming mindful as you perform life's necessary, but mundane, tasks.

• Attentive Driving

Most of us have had the experience of driving our cars as if we were operating under the influence of some unseen "automatic pilot." We lose full consciousness of what we are doing as we explore our thoughts, hold conversations, day-dream, etc. Rarely do we devote significant attention to the actual processes and activities that are involved in driving our car. This exercise enhances our mental discipline during the longer tasks we face such as driving the car.

First, determine that you will use attentive driving *before* you get into the car. Try using it with a short trip that is not during rush hour or in heavy traffic. (It sounds crazy that we shouldn't consider paying full attention to what we are doing in heavy traffic, but as we have become so accustomed to driving without thinking, anything different may seem most alien to us and could serve as a distraction.) Focus your full attention upon *everything* that you do from the moment you insert the key into the door. Become one with what you are doing: your body movements, the decisions that have to be made, the road in front of you, other cars, driving conditions, the vibrations from your car, etc. Keep your attention focused solely upon things related to driving your car. Reject all other thoughts to promote mental discipline.

• Conscious Eating

Many times we eat without any awareness of what we are doing. This not only reduces our potential enjoyment of the food and causes us to eat more than we need, but it also encourages unfocused and undisciplined attention. As in the exercises above, we are to focus our attention fully upon what we are doing. Pay attention to the taste, smell, and texture of the food as you eat. Also concentrate upon the mechanics of eating. Become aware of selecting a bite with the fork or spoon, lifting it to your mouth, and chewing and swallowing the food. If any other thoughts come as you eat, reject them and return your full attention to eating. Continue eating mindfully for the duration of the meal.

How will I know when my mind is cleared of unnecessary thoughts?

Once you have employed the disciplining techniques for use during mediation sessions, you may notice your mind is considerably more calm and centered than before you began. At this point you may want to determine if you still encounter any unnecessary thoughts and sensations which may have to be cleared before continuing with the meditative session. Suggestions for recognizing if unnecessary and potential distracting thoughts remain include determining:

• are you more aware of your inner sensations than your outer sensations?

• are there periods when there seems to be no "thinking" at all, just "being?"

• do you quickly and easily let go of any potentially distracting thoughts or ideas?

• do you experience deep inner peace and tranquility?

• do you experience very little mental imagery of an active, moving nature?

If you experience several of these characteristics, then your mind, most likely, is prepared to continue with the meditative session. If not, then you may need to continue with the same disciplining technique you were employing or select another one. Do not expect to attain a calm, clear mind in every meditation session, *especially in your initial meditative experiences.* It may take considerable practice to attain a centered mind in your meditation sessions. Be patient and diligent in your efforts.

Now that I'm centered, what do I do?

Once you realize that you have cleared your mind through the disciplining techniques, you may continue with your pre–determined purpose for the session including the following:

- staying in the calm, clear awareness you now experience; simply enjoying "being"
- using affirmations to promote a more positive framework for thoughts and attitudes
- using guided visualization exercises (either taped exercises or ones you have learned)
- returning to waking consciousness using the departure technique described above
- continuing on to Step Three

STEP THREE: OBSERVING THE MIND THROUGH RECEPTIVE MEDITATION

GOAL: To develop and enhance meditation skills by observing our own stream of consciousness.

Not only a truer knowledge, but a greater power comes to one in the quietude and silence of a mind that, instead of bubbling on the surface, can go to its own depths and listen.

Sri Aurobindo, *Letters*

When the mind shakes off the many distractions about things which are pressing on it, then the clear meaning of truth appears on it and gives it pledges of genuine knowledge.

St. Maximus, the Confessor, *Chapters on Knowledge*

Rising Bubbles Receptive Meditation

Key Principle: To observe the **process** — not the **actual contents** — of our mind. Our thought processes themselves become the object for contemplation.

Observing the mind through receptive meditation requires that we still the mind and relinquish control over whatever thoughts we select from our own stream of consciousness to be our current reality. We *choose* from this stream of ideas, impressions, and images passing through the mind (even a relaxed, clear mind) those items which will become our reality for the moment simply by paying attention to them and thinking about them. For most people, this selection process is transparent; they are not aware of the stream of consciousness that lies before them or how easily the mind attaches itself to a particular thought. By focusing upon the overall stream of thoughts—and not the actual thoughts flowing along in the stream—receptive meditation enables us to avoid attaching ourselves to our thoughts. Attaching ourselves to any of the thoughts or impressions we select from the stream of consciousness is a significant source of distraction during meditation. Nonattachment to our thoughts is a prerequisite to discovering the ultimate spiritual reality beyond all human thought.

1. Relax and center your mind using any of the techniques above. Once your mind is calm and relaxed, proceed with the receptive meditation.

2. Imagine that you are sitting upon the bottom of a beautiful lake. As this scene is in your imagination, you are quite able to be here. Imagine the cool, refreshing feeling of the water. You feel very comfortable, centered, and relaxed sitting here at the bottom of the lake. Focus upon this image until it is very clear and distinct.

3. Once you have developed a clear image of sitting on the lake's bottom, you begin to notice around you that large air bubbles rise from the bottom. They rise slowly towards the surface. It takes about 6 to 8 seconds for a bubble to form and rise to the surface where they dissipate immediately upon hitting the lake's surface. Just observe the rising bubbles for a few minutes before proceeding with the exercise.

4. After watching bubbles rise for a few minutes, imagine that each thought, idea, sensation, or impression entering your mind becomes a bubble that slowly rises to the lake's surface. Observe the "bubble-thought" for the 6 to 8 seconds that it takes to rise to the surface. Once the thought reaches the surface, **let it go!** Release that thought or sensation completely and return your attention to the bottom of the lake and await the next bubble. If you follow any thoughts longer than the time it takes them to reach the lake's surface, you have become distracted by the thought. Wait patiently for the next thought or image to emerge and let it also become a bubble. Observe it during its trip to the surface. Again, release all attention to it once it reaches the surface.

5. Continue to observe any thought or idea that comes to your attention in this manner for at least 10 minutes. You are not to think about or explore any thought, idea, sensation, or impression any longer than the 6 to 8 seconds it takes the bubble to rise to the lake's surface. If you find yourself dwelling upon any item for longer than this, let it go immediately and return your attention to the bubbles coming from the bottom of the lake.

6. It's all right if your thoughts or images do not make sense or if you see no pattern to your stream of consciousness initially. This exercise requires considerable practice so that we get behind the scenes of the mind to the source from which our awareness flows. Through time and practice, you will get to that point and see innumerable connections and relationships among your thoughts. You can develop more control over your stream of consciousness and learn how to encourage only beneficial mental streams. Be patient! This process takes time, but the rewards are infinite!

Variations

If you are not comfortable sitting upon the lake bottom, imagine sitting upon a desert plateau watching distant smoke signals rise slowly into the air and disappearing in about 6 to

8 seconds. Or, imagine you have a bubble making device in your hands and create bubbles that slowly rise and disappear. Once you find an activity with which you feel comfortable in receptive meditation, stick with it.

One thing is clear form the great minds' perspective: We must transcend all human thought if we desire to know God. Meditation will help us open our minds fully and completely so we can unite with God and Universal Consciousness.

STEP FOUR: TRANSCENDING THE MIND

Consider the following thoughts for a moment:

"My thoughts are not your thoughts declares the Lord."
Isaiah 55: 8

As the air becomes light by the presence of the sun, so are we illumined by the presence of God, and in God's absence we return at once to darkness.
St. Augustine, *The City of God*

Lift up your heart to God…when you first begin, all that you will find is a darkness, a cloud of unknowing; you cannot tell what it is…This darkness and cloud is always between you and God and prevents you from seeing God clearly.
The Cloud of Unknowing

Beyond prayer there is the ineffable vision and ecstasy in the vision, and the hidden mysteries…but there remains an unknowing which is beyond knowledge; though indeed a darkness… it is in this dazzling darkness that the divine things are given to the saints.
St. Gregory of Palamas, *The Triads*

Within the Lotus of the heart God (Brahman) dwells...
meditate on God and you may easily cross the ocean of
darkness. God is pure, the light of light.

Mundaka Upanishad

For those who desire to venture beyond the benefits of
observing the mind as discussed in the previous section,
there is another step in our meditative method. This step,
however, leads us beyond our own minds altogether. It
leads to "God," the ineffable, transcendent being from which
all things flow. Many people from both Eastern and Western
cultures have sought the personal union with God known as
enlightenment, even though each may have had a different
name for the entity they sought. The name really is
inconsequential, for God's true nature cannot be described
by a name or any other term. Words are nothing more than
the tools our ordinary waking consciousness uses to analyze
and categorize, and therefore make intelligible, our
experiences. God, by nature, cannot be experienced directly
by our sense organs. Nor can we experience God by our
own thoughts which are products of our local, conscious
mind. We must experience God transcendentally, beyond all
our sensory and intellectual processes.

Through the ages, many great minds have sought to
experience God transcendentally, with their hearts and not
their heads; however, the direct, personal experience of an
entity whose very nature prevents the human mind from
understanding it has presented a formidable obstacle to their
desires. Many were undaunted by this potential barrier, and
their perseverance and diligence brought them into God's
radiant presence. Despite the many cultural and religious differences among these seekers of enlightenment, their
descriptions (we can *attempt* to explain the union with the
transcendent, even though words are woefully inadequate
for such a purpose) of their experiences bear remarkable
similarities to one another.

Attaining Step Four in our meditation method depends
entirely upon your desire for the personal or transcendental

experience of God. If that is your sincere desire, and you are patient and diligent, then you, too, may experience God directly, just as many great minds have done. Avoid being disheartened or discouraged if you do not obtain immediate results from your efforts. St. Teresa, for example, diligently sought the personal experience of God for twenty years before attaining her heart's desire, and her experience is similar to many others seeking union with God.

There are no definitive "how–to" manuals to help with this journey, although the books and materials on the following page do offer valuable insight. These materials reflect both Eastern and Western ideas on attaining the transcendental experience of God. Perhaps, if your heart is set upon this experience, the best advice would be the ancient Eastern counsel given to those embarking upon a spiritual path:

> # *The journey is the goal.*

Suggested Readings on Meditation

Christianity

- *The Cloud of Unknowing*
- St. John of The Cross, *The Ascent of Mount Carmel*
- St. Julian of Norwich, *Reflections of Divine Love*
- Thomas Merton, *Thoughts in Solitude*
- Jan van Ruusbroec, *The Spiritual Espousals*
- St. Teresa of Avila, *The Interior Castle* and *The Way of Perfection*

Judaism

- *Rabbi Nachman's Wisdom*, translated by Aryeth Kaplan
- *The Zohar*

Buddhism

- Buddha, *Dhammapada*
- Christmas Humphreys, *Concentration and Meditation*
- Thich Nhat Hanh, *The Miracle of Mindfulness*

Taoism

- Daniel Odier, *Nirvana Tao*

Hinduism

Srimad Bhagavatam
Kathopanishad
Yogavasishtha

Sufism

Abu al Najib, *A Sufi Rule for Novices*
Mahmud Shabastri, *The Secret Garden*
Rumi, *Masnavi*

PRELIMINARY GUIDED VISUALIZATION EXERCISES

The nature of mental imagery

In recent years, researchers have probed the nature of mental imagery and the role it plays in our lives. The results, in many instances, are startling, because they offer new perspectives about the ways we actually think and experience the world around us. We now understand that mental imagery influences virtually every aspect of our lives including health, education, the arts, business, and athletics.

Carl Jung describes what happens whenever we concentrate upon a mental image during visualization activities: "It begins to stir, and the unique becomes enriched by details." In other words, as we allow a mental image to develop in our mind, we activate the full power of the image. By concentrating upon the image's details, we trigger numerous mental associations which may not be available from our initial awareness of the image. For example, if you experienced an image of your home at the time you were in high school, you could focus your attention upon this image and its numerous associative details. Most likely other images (high school activities or classes, sports, friends, teachers, etc.) which are associated in your mind with this point in your life also would pop into awareness. The ability to concentrate upon an image so we can trigger associated images is a crucial part of visualization activities.

Mental imagery derives its power from its close relationship to actual life experiences. Mike and Nancy Samuels believe that the words we use in verbal thinking activities are mere labels to describe an experience, while a mental image involves an actual "re–living and re–experiencing" of the experience. The difference is similar to the difference between telling your friends about a new trick you taught your dog versus showing them the trick firsthand. Mental imagery expresses the fullness of our life experiences in ways that words can never communicate. This capability makes mental imagery a crucial part of visualization activities.

Developing visualization skills

Each of us has developed certain visualization capabilities in our responses to life; however, only those people who devote attention to fine–tuning their visualization capabilities will receive the maximum benefits of visualization. Also, each of us experiences mental imagery in different manners such as:

• seeing it in our "mind's eye," either with our eyes open or closed

• seeing it as if it were projected on a screen or blank area in front of our eyes (either open or closed)

• "feeling," but not necessarily seeing, mental images

• seeing colors or black and white images

Unless you have extreme difficulty in experiencing mental imagery, do not worry if you experience these or other variations of mental imagery. Whatever your current experience of mental imagery may be, you can enhance and refine your visualization abilities.

If, however, you do run into difficulty in experiencing imagery, try to pinpoint the cause of the difficulty. Focus upon whatever are your current thoughts and feelings as you prepare for a visualization exercise. Is there anything on your mind which might draw attention away from creating or experiencing imagery? If so, it should be put aside for the time being. Or, perhaps during visualization you are distracted by the "little voice" of your ordinary waking consciousness. If this is the case, withdraw your attention from the verbal chatter and immediately refocus your attention upon the last mental image you experienced. Let that image reappear and begin to explore it.

You also may need to develop a deeper degree of relaxation *prior* to the imagery session to avoid the interruptions caused by verbal chatter. In addition, please do not place any expectations upon what you think you should see during the visualization. Our inner awareness can furnish an ample supply of images appropriate to our needs—if we will learn to give it this freedom. Ready? Then let's begin.

NOTE: Relax using the techniques in the Four Step Meditation Model before you begin this or any other visualization exercise.

CAMERA OBSCURA — PERCY BYSSHE SHELLEY

GOAL: To recall our immediate sensory input which will enhance the clarity and detail of our imagery.

Poet Percy Shelley had a technique which not only sharpened his sensory perception, but also heightened his use of imagery in his writings. Buxton Forman commented in his study of the poet that "Shelley could 'throw a veil over his eyes' and render himself a *camera obscura*." The ability to be a *camera obscura* (a device for capturing an image and projecting it upon a screen) allowed Shelley to reproduce in his mind's eye a scene he had just experienced in such detail that his imagination could render powerful poetic expressions of the experience. You may recognize the similarity between Shelley's technique and the one Whistler used to sharpen his perceptions for his artistic expressions. It is no coincidence that these creative people found this technique to be beneficial to their imaginations. It can be equally beneficial for us as well.

   1. Look at your surroundings and find an object or scene that interests you. Study it with active present tense awareness. Let your eyes scan the object or scene as

you focus upon colors, shading, texture, size, patterns, etc.

2. After you have studied it carefully, close your eyes or look away. Now recall the image as clearly as possible. Explore the image as intensely as you did the object itself. Continue to explore the image until you feel that you have created it in vivid detail in your mind's eye.

3. Open your eyes or look back and compare your mental image with the actual object. Identify any differences that you notice between your image and the object.

4. Repeat the entire process after you consider these differences for a few moments. Continue until your image and the object are almost identical.

ILLUMINATION

GOAL: To develop control over mental imagery.

Occasionally, you may realize that it would be helpful if you could alter or change a mental image in some way. This helps us direct our visualization activities along desirable pathways. In fact, English sculptor Henry Moore proclaimed that he could create vivid images of his sculptural ideas and rotate them in his mind's eye in order to view each potential design from many angles before finalizing his ideas. This exercise promotes our ability to control and alter mental imagery just as Moore did. Practice the exercise until your feel that you have developed enough control over your mental imagery that you can change or alter it at will.

ILLUMINATION: For this exercise you are to imagine a candle burning as it sits on a table in front of you. The candle is at first very dim and the area surrounding it is dark. All you can see is the candle. Then, as you desire it, imagine that the candle slowly becomes brighter. You begin to see the area around the candle and notice the begin to see the area around the candle and notice the objects that are now becoming visible. Whatever you see in the area around the candle is all right. Now focus on these objects and notice their details.

Next, let the candle's light slowly begin to dim. Pay attention to what happens to the area around the candle. See the objects begin to fade from sight. Let the candle return to being just a faint, dim light. Repeat the process a few times alternating between dim and bright illumination. You may want to let whatever objects in the area surrounding the candle appear as they may or you may want to see certain objects appear. You can vary the exercise by using other senses to alter imagery. For example, you could imagine hearing an orchestra playing and speeding it up or slowing it down or changing the tune altogether. Likewise, you could create a "magic garden" in which you control the smell of various plants (a rose that smells like pizza, for example).

NOTE: The following exercises require that you have a degree of control over your mental imagery. If you experience difficulty in creating or controlling your imagery, continue to practice the exercises in the previous section before proceeding with the exercises in this unit. Also, to ensure that your mind is relaxed and disciplined enough to benefit from these exercises, complete Step Two of the Four Step Meditation Model before you attempt any of the following exercises.

ENERGY BUBBLE VISUALIZATION

GOAL: To create a energy bubble that can be used for specific healing or energizing activities.

1. Place your hands about six inches apart in front of you with the palms facing each other. Close your eyes if you like.

2. Imagine that a warm globe of beautiful golden energy forms between your palms. Feel its warmth and energy growing in intensity until it feels as if you had an actual object between your palms. Imagine trying to push your palms together and feeling the resistance the globe produces. Continue experiencing this energy globe until you feel ready to use it for healing or energizing activities as suggested below.

HEALING: If you experience a pain or ache anywhere in your body, the energy bubble can be used to promote healing. Move your hands and the bubble towards the location of the pain. Gently massage the energy bubble into the area where the pain is concentrated. Use your thought power to sense the golden energy warming and easing the pain. Let this sensation continue for a few minutes as you visualize the golden healing energy at work. Feel the relief that this energy brings.

ENERGIZING: If your body is tired and lacks energy, use the golden energy globe to revitalize your body. Move the energy globe into an area experiencing tiredness. Feel it restoring the body's natural energy balance. Imagine a warm tingling sensation as the energy globe revitalizes any or all parts of your body. If you feel mentally drained or exhausted, move the energy globe into your head and let it energize your mind. Your thought power creates the energy globe and enables it to restore energy to your body and mind.

THE INNER GUIDE VISUALIZATION — CARL JUNG

GOAL: To contact your personal Inner Guide and seek his or her wisdom for your own needs.

Carl Jung wrote in his autobiographical book, *Memories, Dreams, Reflections*, that he often consulted his inner guide named Philemon for advice: "Philemon represented a force which was not myself...I held conversations with him, and he said things which I had not previously thought. For I observed that it was he who spoke, not I...Psychologically, Philemon represented superior insight." Jung found that by creating an inner guide with whom he could communicate that he could stimulate his thinking and broaden his perspectives upon life issues. Jung was not the only great mind consulting with an inner guide as Socrates also had an inner guide with whom he frequently communicated.

You, like these great minds, have inner guides waiting to assist with your self–realization activities. An inner guide, as Jung mentioned, represents superior insight from your own unconscious mind or from the universal mind. Your conscious, or small, mind addresses ordinary daily activities and often is unaware of insights that your unconscious mind may have to offer you. Creating a mental image of an inner guide "personalizes" the insights and helps make them more accessible to the conscious mind. Your inner guide can reveal insights that otherwise may remain unconscious and unavailable for your growth. Suggestions for communicating with your inner guide are below.

Characteristics of your Inner Guide

• The Inner Guide always will be a human being, although not necessarily a real person (he or she may be a literary or mythological character).

• He or she may or may not be someone you know, either personally or by reputation.

• Your Inner Guide represents some aspect of yourself (including, according to Jung, the universal wisdom of your collective unconscious) that your conscious mind may not understand at this time.

• Your Inner Guide may talk with you, ask or answer questions, present you with a symbol or abstract image, have insights and ideas to present you, or just may appear and "be" there with you.

• You actually may have several inner guides, and the one that appears on any occasion may not be the one you had expected or hoped might appear. Or, on some occasions, more than one may appear during the same visualization session.

Contacting your Inner Guide

1. Relax for a few moments in a comfortable, quiet location. Use the relaxation and mental disciplining techniques from the Four Step Meditation Model.

2. Once you have calmed and focused your mind, then imagine you are in a beautiful meadow looking into a clear pool of water before you. See yourself in the clear water and pay attention to your reflection until you "feel" your Inner Guide has arrived by your side. Whenever you feel that your Inner Guide has appeared, slowly turn to face your Inner Guide and begin to sense him or her using visual and kinesthetic sensory awareness (visualize clothing, facial expression, or body position; touch his or her clothing, hand, or shoulder).

3. Once you feel your Inner Guide to be there with you in the visualization, pause for a few moments to see if he or she has any comments, symbolic images, or questions to offer you. If your Inner Guide has a comment or symbol to offer, accept whatever it is openly and willingly, asking for clarification if you feel you need it. If he or she asks you a question, let the first response that enters your mind be your answer. Do not try to construct a response, let it just happen without any conscious effort. Allow your Inner Guide to receive your answer and pause to see his or her response before attempting any other action.

4. After your initial exchange, ask your Inner Guide a question or ask if there is anything else he or she would

like to say or do at this time. Wait for a response. If there is additional communication, be open to it. If not, you may just "be" there with your guide for a few moments, or you may want to say farewell for this encounter. Always bid farewell to your Inner Guide and thank him or her for the insight you have received.

5. Whenever you sense that it is time to return to active waking consciousness, slowly count backwards from five to one. When you reach one, say to yourself: "I am relaxed, refreshed, and mentally alert." Then slowly open your eyes.

Exploring your experience

1. Record your immediate impressions of the experience in your journal. Indicate what you experienced and any insights that are apparent at this time.

2. Draw any symbolic imagery your Inner Guide provided you. Record in your journal any insights that are apparent at this time.

3. If there is something that you do not understand and you feel the need for additional information, consider the following methods:

   • Phrase a question to ask at the next encounter with your Inner Guide.

   • Phrase a question, put it on a notecard, and place it where you will encounter it frequently during the day. Await an answer or insight.

   • Draw your immediate impression of anything that you do not understand and place it where you will encounter it frequently. Await an answer or insight.

   • Mold in clay or Play–doh your immediate impressions and see if insight arrives.

EXERCISES:
WHAT THEN MUST WE DO?

From the elementary awareness of the amoeba, through the increased awareness of the invertebrates, to the uniquely self–aware consciousness of the human, the evolutionary path has been characterized by a trend of increasing awareness.

Willis Harman, *Higher Creativity*

We attribute the advent of the "self–fulfilling prophecy" to the mythical Greek sculptor Pygmalion, who, in his yearning to find a suitable wife, caused one of his statues to come to life. The image he held in his mind ultimately became his reality. Willis Harman acknowledges what great minds have known for centuries—that self–fulfilling prophecies are not the mere substance of myth; rather, they can have a profound effect upon our lives. Harman believes that: "Our beliefs, conscious and unconscious, create the future in ways more subtle and more powerful than we ordinarily take into account." We *literally* have the power to create the future. Granted, modern materialistically inspired science gives us the power to alter the genetic code, disrupt the biosphere, and affect physical reality in a plethora of other ways; however, the ability to create the future is not limited to the handiwork of science.

The ancient Greeks, like their counterparts from the East, understood how influential our minds can be in creating reality. These great minds seldom have seen humanity as a passive entity held hostage to the whims of a mechanistic universe. Instead, they have seen us as *active participants* in the unfolding of a grand, universal plan that often escapes our ordinary waking consciousness' understanding. Today, modern science is beginning to acknowledge what great minds intuitively have known—that our thoughts are the blueprints for the future.

Earlier in this century, William James maintained that we are the sole architects of our destiny, and as such, if we change our inner mental attitudes, then we change outer material reality. Unfortunately, in our role as architects, we have not been as judicious as we could have been in creating our relationship with each other or the universe. Our true inner nature is innately spiritual, universal, and eternal. On the other hand, our outer physical nature, as it is both temporal and finite, often reflects little of our true inner nature. We, therefore, experience a discrepancy or void between our innately spiritual true nature and our personally "manufactured" outer nature.

In our rush to fill this void with *something* so that we do not feel our lives are hollow or meaningless, we often have turned to materialistic gratification, rather than spiritual enrichment. Socrates lamented during his trial that the citizens of the great city of Athens squandered their opportunity to nourish and develop their souls through their preoccupations with power, money, and status. Likewise, St. Francis, Buddha, the Hebrew prophets Jeremiah and Isaiah, Confucius, Lao Tzu, Jesus, St. Teresa, Mohammed, Thoreau, Gandhi, and many other great minds have pleaded for us to restore the proper spiritual perspective to our lives. Filling the void that exists between our true nature and our manufactured self with the temporal, transitory, and essentially unfulfilling products of material reality, prevents us from assuming our true roles as active participants in the universal plan. It also pushes the world precariously close to total oblivion.

The Crossing Point by M. C. Richards describes our attempts to fill our inner void with materialistic gratification as being inherently misguided, because materialistic pleasures, due to their transitory nature, can in no way satisfy inner spiritual hunger. Our increased potential for awareness, as discussed by Harman, now allows us to see more clearly than ever that seeking materialistic solutions to spiritual hunger is both counterproductive and destructive. It is an urge to scratch an insatiable itch that offers no relief for the source of irritation.

Paradoxically, parallel to our evolutionary increase in consciousness, there has been an increased drive to conquer the material universe. This drive has shifted our endowed responsibilities as stewards for creation to that of exploiters of creation. Many primitive cultures have reflected the idea that humans, as the most advanced element of creation, are to serve as nurturers, as protectors, of the universal bounty afforded us by God. Instead, modern "civilized" societies have seemed more intent to dismantle creation in our fruitless efforts to quench our spiritual hunger with material resources. Living well, indeed, has become the best revenge for not being able to fulfill our spiritual needs.

Continuing upon this path to satisfy our needs could lead to the demise of our planet and all its myriad lifeforms maintains Frances Vaughan in her book, *The Inward Arc*. She stresses that we must face current human threats to planetary survival immediately, if we and other lifeforms are to endure. We really have little choice other than to relinquish our pointless materialistic manipulation of the Earth and seek instead a true and harmonious relationship with the universe. This relationship cannot develop, however, as long as we are preoccupied with materialistic pleasures. If we desire to utilize the benefits that our increasing awareness has provided us, then we must redirect our inner longings towards the only means that can satisfy them—our true spiritual nature.

Granted, this is no small task. But if your inner awareness communicates to you the urgency of this dilemma, then any delay or denial of the actions you could take to reorder your priorities and redirect them towards spiritual enrichment would further compound the problem. Philosopher and theologian Teilhard de Chardin writes in *The Phenomenon of Man* that, for the human race, "the only way forward is in the direction of a common passion." All across the planet—at this very moment—people are awakening to their true nature and addressing their spiritual priorities. They are discovering that the true meaning of life is not to be found in the material by–products of creation; rather, it can be found only in creation itself!

There are many constructive actions you could initiate to join forces with others who are dedicated to our spiritual awakening. These efforts not only will enhance your relationship with yourself and the universe, but also will affect the process on a global level. For as Teilhard maintains: "A truth once seen, even by a single mind, always ends by imposing itself on the totality of human consciousness." Perhaps the truth you uncover today in your search for spiritual enlightenment is just what has been needed all along by people around you. Your truth may awaken them out of a materialistic slumber and help them re–orient their priorities towards more spiritual ends.

Suggestions to Develop Spiritual Priorities

1. Meditation and Contemplative Prayer. There simply is no better way to unlock and activate your spiritual nature than through the same method used by great minds through the ages in their personal search for enlightenment. *Meditate daily*. Also, join with others, on occasion, to unite your meditative energies and send them where they may be needed. For example, each New Year's Day Eve, at noon Greenwich Time, millions of people around the world unite in an hour of meditation to promote peace and harmony on Earth. Other group meditations are directed towards similar spiritual aims. Unite your true spiritual nature with others and experience the power that is ours to claim.

2. Do not accept negative images of the future. Certainly many great minds have portrayed potential future realities as being essentially hopeless and bleak. We only have to turn to Huxley's *Brave New World* or Orwell's *1984* to experience how meaningless life could become by our continued pursuit of materialistic ends. The authors have not written these stories to say how the future *actually will be;* instead, they only tell us what *could happen* if we don't change our priorities. Sociologist Fred Polak conducted an exhaustive study of many once–prominent civilizations that have somehow managed to decline from their zenith. His book, *Images of the Future,* concluded that: "As long as a society's image is positive and flourishing, the flower of culture is in full bloom. Once the image begins to decay and lose its vitality, however, the culture does not long survive."

It would be pointless—and potentially harmful—to elucidate the endless assortment of negative imagery that modern culture now beams towards us. Politicians and the mass media are not the only culprits. There also are many prophets of doom within the religious ranks who tell us the end is near and that God's full wrath and fury will soon be unleashed upon us. Such soothsayers, even though they may seek spiritual rebirth for each of us, have focused their attention far too prominently upon material and not spiritual reality. Their "wisdom" is not upon the same plane as the wisdom from great minds. Great minds always have known that, if we desire to become more spiritual, we must center our attention upon positive spiritual images such as love, peace, and harmony and not upon negative images such as destruction, judgment, or sin. We achieve more success through creating positive images of what we desire than through creating negative ones of what we hope to avoid.

3. Affirm a positive future. Do not focus upon the horrors that could befall us. Activate the unlimited power of your mind and join with others to create the future that God intends for us. Use affirmations such as the following daily:

• I am filled with a sense of peace about the future.

• I accept my role as part of a spiritual renaissance.

• Each day I am more positive about the future.

• I am part of God's plan for a positive, harmonious future.

4. Act as if your every action influences the future. Centuries ago Immanuel Kant wrote what he called "the Categorical Imperative." Kant realized that if we truly desire to improve our future, then we must assume responsibility for its development. By acting as if everything you did actually influenced the future, you would tend to reflect more upon your actions, thereby leading you towards more harmonious relationships with others and the universe. The Categorical Imperative, since it recognizes both the power of our minds and of our actions, can guide our efforts to create a positive future.

5. Understand the nature of a spiritual life. Henry Thoreau and Leo Tolstoy are two modern great minds who have struggled with the nature of living a spiritual life. Their works portrayed the difficulty that humanity faces in its efforts to subdue our lower, more instinctual nature and turn, instead, for guidance from our higher, more spiritual nature. Likewise, in this century, Schweitzer and Gandhi have been instrumental in resolving the fray between our animalistic and spiritual natures. If we increase our understanding of what constitutes a spiritual life, then we, too, may begin to resolve this age–old battle between our two natures. You may wish to complete the Spiritual Path Self–assessment which follows this chapter to gain more insight into what a spiritual life entails.

There is, perhaps, no better way to end this book than with the timeless wisdom of Albert Schweitzer. In his college days, Schweitzer became a world–class organist and earned a doctorate in music history. He toured Europe and stunned audiences with his musical performances. Then, one day at age thirty, because he had learned to listen to and trust the spiritual presence within him, Schweitzer's whole world changed. His inner spiritual voice instructed him to leave the concert halls, enter medical school, and be ready to sail for Africa upon graduation. Schweitzer willingly obeyed, and, as a result of his willingness to follow the voice within him, he altered the future, not only his future, but also the entire world's future. We may not have to forsake our present careers or put aside our present reality as Schweitzer did; however, we must heed his advice:

"I don't know what your destiny will be, but one thing I know: the only ones among you who will be truly happy are those who will have sought and found how to serve."

WALKING THE SPIRITUAL PATH

1. What does it mean to be spiritual?

- To be spiritual means seeking wisdom from the essence of things, not from their surface or appearance.
- To be spiritual means seeking to create your life with guidance from a source greater than your local mind, your ordinary waking consciousness.
- To be spiritual means not being influenced by the world's changing values.
- To be spiritual means nonattachment to material or sensual pleasures.
- To be spiritual means seeking to live a fully productive life, a life employing your talents to meet the needs of others.
- To be spiritual means choosing to do those things or think those thoughts that contribute meaning to life and avoiding thoughts or actions that do not.
- To be spiritual is to accept your calling to activate your highest spiritual nature.

2. What are the characteristics of a person on a spiritual path?

- Someone who devotes as much time and energy to spiritual growth as to career, recreational, and family matters.

- Someone who develops their "inner voice" to the point they can distinguish it from their ego.

- Someone who actively works to find balance in life through meditation, dreamwork, or spiritual counseling activities.

- Someone who lives in the "now."

- Someone who seeks to profit only from business activities that are honorable, blameless, and do not harm to others.

- Someone who loves others as they love themselves.

- Someone who devotes themselves to experiencing increasingly higher levels of divine involvement in their life.

Take a few moments to perform the following self–assessment of your present commitment to a spiritual path. List what you consider to be your present strengths and weaknesses for living a more spiritual life. Use more space, if necessary. Use the results to guide the journey ahead.

Present Strengths   **Present Weaknesses**

BIBLIOGRAPHY:
SECRETS FROM GREAT MINDS

Please Note: As much as it was possible, sources for the quotations by the great minds were identified in the text. Various editions and translations of their works are available, and you are encouraged to go to those sources. The following bibliographic listings provide a foundation for further study.

Readings by and about the Great Minds

Aristotle, *Poetics, Metaphysics, and Nicomachean Ethics*

Marcus Aurelius, *Meditations*, various editions

J. E. Brown, *The Spiritual Legacy of the American Indian,* NY, Crossroad Publ, 1987.

Martin Buber, *I and Thou*, various editions

Richard M.Bucke, *Cosmic Consciousness,* New York, Causeway Books, 1974.
Buddha, *Dhammapada*, Berkeley, Dharma Publishing,1985

Confucius, *The Analects*

Ralph Waldo Emerson, *Essays* and *Journals*

Lao Tzu, *Tao Tê Ching* (numerous translations)

Thomas Merton, *Contemplative Prayer* and *Thoughts in Solitude*, Doubleday, 1971

Plato, *Apology, Euthyphro, Phaedo, and Crito (main texts about Socrates) and Republic*

Plotinus, *The Enneads and On Intellectual Beauty*, (various translations)
G. Reale, *From the Origins to Socrates: History of Ancient Philosophy*, SUNY–Albany, 1987

Kathleen J. Regier, *The Spiritual Image in Modern Art,* Wheaton, IL, Theosophical Publ, 1987

Percy Bysshe Shelley, *A Defence of Poetry*

Henry David Thoreau, *Walden and Journals*

Poetry of Wordsworth, Blake, Byron, Shelley, Dickinson, Tennyson, Whitman, Basho, Bunan, and Yeats

Spiritual Texts

Bible, Koran, Bhagavadgita, Cloud of Unknowing, Upanishads, Talmud, Rig Veda, and various writings of St Teresa, St Thomas, St Augustine, Meister Eckhart, St John of the Cross, and Zen and Sufi Masters

Creative Illumination, Dreams, and Intuition

José Argüelles, *The Transformative Vision*, Shambhala, 1975

Patricia Garfield, *Creative Dreaming*, Ballantine, 1976

Jacques Maritain, *Creative Intuition in Art and Poetry*, Princeton University Press, 1981

Frances Vaughan, *Awakening Intuition,* Doubleday, 1979

Strephon Williams, *The Jungian-Senoi Dreamwork Manual*, Journey Press-1, 1985

Ellen Winner, *Invented Worlds: The Psychology of the Arts*, Harvard Univ. Press, 1982

Psychology, Self-Actualization, and Evolution of Consciousness

Sri Aurobindo, *The Life Divine*, Lotus Light, Wilmot, Wisconsin, 1980

Erich Fromm, *To Have or To Be* and *The Art of Loving*, various editions

Stanislav Grof, *Human Survival and Consciousness Evolution*, SUNY–Albany , 1988

Willis Harman, *Global Mind Change*, Indianapolis,
· Knowledge Systems Inc., 1988

William James, *Varieties of Religious Experience*

Carl Jung, *Modern Man in Search of a Soul* and *Memories,
Dreams, and Reflections*

Abraham Maslow, *The Further Reaches of Human Nature*,
Esalen, 1971

Lewis Mumford, *The Transformation of Man*, Harper and
Brothers, 1956

Carl Rogers, *On Becoming a Person*

Peter Russell, *The Global Brain,* Tarcher, 1983

Pierre Teilhard de Chardin, *The Phenomenon of Man, and
The Future of Man*, Harper & Row

Paul Tillich, *The Courage to Be*, Yale Univ Press, 1952

Modern Science and Ancient Wisdom

David Bohm, *Wholeness and the Implicate Order*, Routledge
and Kegan Paul Ltd, 1980

David Bohm and David Peat, *Science, Order, and Creativity*,
Bantam, 1987

Niels Bohr, *Essays, 1958—1962, Atomic Physics and
Human Knowledge*, Wiley, 1963

Fritjof Capra, *The Tao of Physics*

J.Hayward, *Perceiving Ordinary Magic: Science and
Intuitive Wisdom*, Shambhala, 1984

P. Vitz and A. Glimcher, *Modern Art and Modern Science*,
Praeger, 1984

Ken Wilber, ed., *The Holographic Paradigm*, Shambhala,
1982

Ken Wilber ed., *Quantum Questions*, Shambhala, 1984

Gary Zukav, *The Dancing Wu Li Masters*, various